GET IT DONE!

Beat Procrastination and Achieve Better Work-Life Balance! Boost Your productivity And Work Smarter Using The 80/20 Principle!

Philip I. Snyder

Copyright © 2021 by Dream Books LLC
All rights reserved.

The content contained within this book may not be reproduced, duplicated or transmitted without direct written permission from the author or the publisher. Under no circumstances will any blame or legal responsibility be held against the publisher, or author, for any damages, reparation, or monetary loss due to the information contained within this book. Either directly or indirectly. You are responsible for your own choices, actions, and results.

Legal Notice:

This book is copyright protected. This book is only for personal use. You cannot amend, distribute, sell, use, quote or paraphrase any part, or the content within this book, without the consent of the author or publisher.

Disclaimer Notice:

Please note the information contained within this document is for educational and entertainment purposes only. All effort has been executed to present accurate, up to date, and reliable, complete information. No warranties of any kind are declared or implied. Readers acknowledge that the author is not engaging in the rendering of legal, financial, medical or professional advice. The content within this book has been derived from various sources. Please consult a licensed professional before attempting any techniques outlined in this book. By reading this document, the reader agrees that under no circumstances is the author responsible for any losses, direct or indirect, which are incurred as a result of the use of the information contained within this document, including, but not limited to,
— errors, omissions, or inaccuracies.

Table of Contents

Introduction 7
The Problem of Procrastination 11
But what causes it? 12
How Procrastination Manifests 16
What Does Being Unproductive Mean? 17
Chapter I The Psychology Behind Why We Procrastinate 25
Dealing with Negative Emotions 26
The Irony of Procrastination 28
The Intention and Action Gap 30
Neuropsychology of Procrastination 33
Why Do People Procrastinate? 35
Chapter II Dissecting Procrastination in Daily Life 43
What Procrastination and Productivity Aren't 44
Mood Regulation 47
When We Fail to Regulate Our Emotions 50
Motivation (and De-Motivation) 53
Meeting Your Future Self 54
Time-Wasters: What Contributes to Our Procrastination? 56
Taking Control 59
Chapter III Our Unproductive Habits 67
The Faces of Procrastination and Unproductiveness 69
Which of these Procrastinators Are You? 75
The Psychology of Productivity 76
How to Know If you are a Chronic Procrastinator? 80
Chapter IV Busy, but Not Productive 83
Why Being Busy is Not Ideal 84
Busyness vs. Productivity 87

Effectiveness vs. Efficiency: What's the Difference? 92
"Multitasking" And How It Hurts Your Productivity 94
Chapter V The Pitfalls of Perfectionism.......................... 99
What is Perfectionism? 100
Why Perfection Works Against Productivity 103
The Stigma of Failure.. 107
Curbing Perfectionism... 109
The Failure Test... 113
Chapter VI The Magic of Good Habits 117
Why Good Habits Matter 118
What Productivity Looks Like... 121
Chapter VII Productivity Boost Using the 80/20 Principle 143
What is the 80/20 Principle? 145
Implementing the 80/20 Principle..................................... 149
How NOT to Apply the 80/20 Rule.................................. 157
Chapter VIII Better Done than Perfect 161
Adjusting the Perfectionist Mindset 162
Embracing Imperfections 167
Chapter IX Walking The Work-Life Balance Tightrope 181
How Can the Balance Boost Your Productivity? 186
Better Work-Life Balance for Higher Productivity 190
Chapter X Maintaining and Tweaking Your Progress .. 201
Closing Remarks.. 209
Resources 219

Other books by Dream Books LLC

"500 Funny Quotes for Women"

"500 Funny Quotes for Men"

"Mark Twain Quotes of Wit and Wisdom"

INTRODUCTION

"Only put off until tomorrow what you are willing to die having left undone"

Pablo Picasso

INTRODUCTION

You might think procrastination is a problem of the modern age when the internet and smartphones allow us to spend countless hours doing nothing. But believe it or not, human beings have struggled with procrastination since ancient times. In an Egyptian hieroglyph from 1400 B.C. and translated by Professor Ronald Leprohon of the University of Toronto, it reads, *"Friend, stop putting off work and allow us to go home in good time."* Around 800 B.C., another proclamation against procrastination appears in *Work and Days*, a poem by the Greek poet Hesiod, he warns his brother as follows:

> *Do not put your work off till to-morrow and the day after; for a sluggish worker does not fill his barn, nor one who puts off his work: industry makes work go well, but a man who puts off work is always at hand-grips with ruin.*

A little closer to us in the 1400s, Geoffrey Chaucer, in one of his Canterbury Tales, advises us, *"…the goodness you may do this day, do it; and delay it not until the morrow."* Great advice! Too bad Chaucer did not practice what he preached since he completed only twenty-four of the one hundred Canterbury tales he planned to write before death!

You could even say that things have just gotten worse in recent years with the advent of new, convenient technologies. But that does not mean to say that fewer people were procrastinating decades or centuries ago.

Being a "waiter" instead of a "doer" is a temptation that people have always had.

Does any of these examples sound familiar to you?

- Wanting to start a new healthy habit such as exercising or dieting, but delaying it until you are in a better mood.

- Promising yourself to start the hobby you always wanted to try but postponing the decision until you feel more motivated.

- Planning to start a new side hustle to generate more cash but wasting time watching inspirational videos

- Starting to learn your favorite foreign language but postponing it until you have more free time

- Wanting to clean the house this Saturday but spending the whole day on Netflix and Facebook

If any of the examples mentioned above (or countless other instances where we put off tasks) sound familiar, take comfort in the fact that you are not alone. Procrastination is a sensation that has been affecting many of us. In fact, we all procrastinate from time to time. Things become complicated when procrastination becomes a way of life, affecting all aspects of an individual's life; their work, relationships, physical and mental health, etc. According to the data published by the American Psychological Association, around 20% of adult Americans are chronic procrastinators. That is higher than the number of people diagnosed with any mental or physical health issue.

Then again, there are people out there who have managed to stick by an internal set of rules and get things done efficiently. Better yet, some are doing more and can get a lot of things done within a single day without sacrificing quality (and their sanity).

Is this possible? The short answer is Yes. The long answer? Overcoming procrastination is a systemic process that will require significant changes in key aspects of your life. How you go about dealing with procrastination and improving on your productivity will involve a comprehensive plan that includes practical, actionable strategies as well as tips to sustain and build on your improvements.

For most people, there are two major obstacles to getting things done:

1. Getting started: This is where procrastination comes into the picture, i.e., all those habits and tricks we use to put tasks off.

2. Finishing the task and getting the desired result within a reasonable time: This is where productivity matters, i.e., getting things done effectively and efficiently.

This book is, in essence, about overcoming procrastination and improving productivity. It intends to help you develop your tailor-made plan to address both of these issues and to reach your personal and professional life goals easier and faster.

The Problem of Procrastination

Procrastination is delaying or putting tasks off to a later time. Experts describe procrastination as "a failure of self-regulation brought about by the irrational delay of performing tasks despite knowing the negative consequences that could arise from such." If that definition is a bit too complicated, here's something more straightforward: It is the act of putting things off despite knowing how important it is for you to complete such tasks. It is as if the brain's rational part cannot make decisions because it is overwhelmed by an inner child who is a handful and very naughty! That naughty inner child is our procrastinating desire to get instant gratification by watching YouTube videos or browsing the Internet or social media instead of getting our to-do list done.

As was stated before, procrastination is something endemic in us. No matter who you are or how organized you think you are, you might have found yourself performing minor or trivial tasks while holding off on more important ones. As the saying goes, "Everyone procrastinates, but not everyone is a procrastinator." Here, "procrastinators" are that 20% of the American population (or perhaps roughly the same number elsewhere) who are chronically delaying their life. Since procrastination is a mental crutch, its effect is far-reaching. It will affect every aspect of one's life that requires considerable thought, effort, and dedication. Whether at home, school, or work, procrastination can prevent us from reaching our goals, create stress, affect our relationships, and much more.

But what causes it?

We will delve deeper into the causes of procrastination in later chapters. It is crucial to understand that the problem has roots in the very way we think and perceive the world around us.

To better understand this, here's a scenario: Let us say that your boss just gave you an important project with due date in two weeks. A quick look at the project details made you exclaim, "Ha! I can finish this in a day or two. I'll start working on this next week". But then, as you start working next week, you realized why your boss gave you two weeks. Our tendency to lull ourselves into a false sense of security has often leads us to put things off until the last minute.

Dealing with challenging emotions can also be another source of procrastination. Emotions such as boredom, anxiety, stress, and sadness could paralyze us and prevent us from getting started on our to-do list. Our minds (and sometimes our bodies) should first manage to control these emotions to begin working afterward. Hence, we often procrastinate because we fail at regulating our feelings.

One of the core concepts that you will learn about in this book is the need to be in the "proper" frame of mind to be productive. It is also essential to realize that procrastination and lack of productivity are not because of laziness. Each person has several reasons for procrastination and lack of productivity. Let's discuss some of the more common ones.

1. Heavy Work Loads

Procrastination tends to increase in output-reliant environments like school and work. An analysis in 2007 by the Psychological Bulletin found that procrastination is very prevalent in academic environments. In fact, 80-90% of students put off doing coursework regularly. In areas where people are required to produce something for either income or a passing grade, the following habits are often seen:

- Overestimating available time to perform tasks.
- Underestimating the time needed for a task.
- Wrongly assuming that a task can be done once a person is in the right mindset.

2. Mental Conditions

Aside from how a brain is hardwired to perceive and process information, a person can also have mental conditions that prevent them from getting things done as quickly as possible. Here are some notable examples:

A. Depression

The general feeling of hopelessness and helplessness and a considerable lack of mental energy can make it challenging to start on tasks even with prior experience on those tasks. Depression can also lead to periods of doubt and insecurity in performing specific tasks. As such, a person tends to gravitate more on actions that their mind will feel comfortable performing while under this condition.

B. Obsessive-Compulsive Disorders (OCD)

The tendency to put off important tasks is also relatively high in people that suffer from forms of Obsessive-Compulsive disorders. OCD is a condition that is linked to an unhealthy form of perfectionism. Focusing too much on getting things 100% right makes the mind dawdle until it fails to start a task. A person with OCD often deals with indecision. Thus, addressing this need is key to motivating the person to become more decisive and proactive.

C. Attention-Deficit Hyperactive Disorder (ADHD)

Attention-Deficit Hyperactive Disorder is also one of the reasons why a person will suffer from procrastination. This is because ADHD functions by assaulting the mind with so many stimuli that it cannot ignore. Thus, those who deal with OCD often find it hard to focus on one important task, which leads to low output quality. That is provided, of course, if one even manages to finish a task.

3. Other Reasons

Aside from deep psychological reasons, there are other minor reasons we can't start or finish important tasks, such as the following:

- Not understanding what must be done
- Lack of knowledge on how to do specific tasks
- Lack of desire to do something
- Lack of care in the value of a task
- Not "in the mood" to do tasks

- The tendency to do things "in the last minute"
- Forgetfulness
- Lack of initiative
- The tendency to wait for the "right moment"
- Inefficient Multi-tasking
- Paralysis by Analysis

These are just some of the reasons why a person tends to fail to complete or start certain tasks. We will discuss in more detail later on how your brain is hardwired to think when it comes to performing specific tasks.

Thus, by understanding how your brain works, you know how you could overcome the mental hurdles towards productivity. You might even be surprised to find out how these reasons correlate with each other, which could help you develop comprehensive lifestyle changes.

How Procrastination Manifests

So, how is procrastination being done? Believe it or not, all forms of procrastination can fall under two categories. First, there is the type of procrastination that comes from being unable to decide and act on that decision. This is what we call Passive Procrastination. Second, there is the type when we deliberately put things off because we feel that we produce the best results under pressure. This is called Active Procrastination.

For now, these concepts might be a bit hard to understand. Do not worry, though, as this book will help you grasp when you might be actively or passively putting things off.

Before proceeding, you should realize that you are procrastinating when you:

- Hold off on completing a task out of fear that it does not meet a standard.
- Put off tasks because you tend to overlook details.
- Do not believe in the concept of following a schedule.
- Do not perform tasks out of fear that it is new and unfamiliar to you.
- Consume too much time to do a task that could be done in a shorter period.

In short, procrastination is that you either cannot decide to do something or fail to perform it on time.

What Does Being Unproductive Mean?

Getting started is a crucial step in getting things done, but it is often not enough. We need to finish the task with acceptable quality and within a reasonable time. This is essential in all venues of life but is especially crucial for success in a profession.

INTRODUCTION

Many think that being productive is all about being busy, but that is not necessarily true. In fact, some people hide behind busy schedules to avoid doing work. Busyness for the sake of being busy is not essentially a healthy habit. It could even contribute towards an unproductive lifestyle if left unchecked.

Instead, productivity is about delivering results at the right time and in the best possible quality. That could be a problem in the rather hectic pace of work these days. With emails here, meetings there, and every sort of technological distraction readily available at your hands, maintaining focus on one task at a time is becoming a challenge.

There are also quite a lot of productivity killers out there. Social media, the inability to say No, the tendency towards multi-tasking, no set priorities, and perfectionism are just a few examples. It would help if you realized that our minds run on a relatively finite source called willpower. If our will is spent on trivial pursuits, little will be left to make critical decisions.

Before we continue, it is essential to note that it does not really help focus on being 100% productive. What matters more is to have a reasonably high level of productivity and maintain a healthy work-life balance. Once procrastination is under control and productivity is high, it will be possible to meet deadlines, deliver results, and fend off unnecessary stress. In this way, the work-life balance and, along with it, productivity will improve.

Procrastination is more than just a time problem. It impacts your overall philosophy toward living. In as much as procrastination is a mental hurdle, its effects are nonetheless physical. The most obvious example of this is the quality of work that you put out. By rushing things through, you sacrifice quality. As such, that passing grade or promotion you were seeking might be compromised.

However, the effects of procrastination do not only affect your major, long-term goals. It could even affect how you conduct yourself daily.

Some of the more direct effects of putting things off include:

- Not paying bills on time.
- Dealing with a massive crowd on sales since you waited for too long to buy stuff for the holidays.
- Getting in trouble with the Internal Revenue Service because you failed to file your Income Tax Returns on time.
- Missing out on time with your family or friends to deal with work backlog.

Of course, these are just minor stuff. You would also have to deal with more massive, life-altering consequences, for example:

- Coping with high-stress levels

- Resentment from your co-workers, family, friends, and other social relationships.
- Problems with delinquent payments and documents.

You will later find out that the consequences of procrastination do worsen the longer it is not addressed. It could lead you to even more opportunities to procrastinate in the future. It's a rather tall order. Is it really possible to make a complete lifestyle change towards higher productivity? The answer is yes!

The best way to start addressing these problems is to identify why they occur in the first place. What makes you tick? Why do you put off specific tasks? The book will guide you by understanding yourself and finding why you cannot get things done ASAP. Once these mental hurdles are identified, the next thing to do is developing productivity habits. This is why addressing procrastination and non-productivity requires system and repetition. You have to condition your mind to perform at a certain level and prevent it from going back to its sloppy ways.

Thus, this book aims to help you do two main themes:

A. Changing from a waiter to a doer and get started on things.

B. Finish the tasks with the results and the time that you want.

The first theme focuses on procrastination. We all procrastinate from time to time. But once procrastination becomes a habit and we do it all the time, it could become a significant productivity pitfall. The second theme is more about productivity. Getting started is excellent but not enough. We need to get the intended task done with acceptable quality and within a reasonable time. Once we get started, it is essential to finish the task effectively, with the minimum possible effort. Is all of this possible, though? Has anyone actually managed to do more out of their time without sacrificing quality?

You might be surprised to hear that, yes, overcoming procrastination is not only possible but sustainable as well. Wouldn't it be great if you could also find ways to make yourself more productive while also reducing stress and anxiety?

In this book, you can also discover simple yet effective strategies to make yourself productive while also managing the stress associated with constant action. You will find out that dealing with productivity is more than just addressing why you are procrastinating in the first place. It's about adopting a lifestyle that lets you do more while also finding ways to deal with stress regularly.

How do we go about turning you from an indecisive procrastinator to a go-getter? The book does so in three phases. First, you need to **understand why you fail to get things done**. What is holding you back? Is it something that you tend to do or think? Or is it something external that prevents you from optimizing how you go about your day-to-day living?

Second, you have to understand **how you fail at getting things done.** Your habits, the way you make your schedules (if you have them, of course), and even your environments' physical setup can hinder your productivity levels. Understanding how your brain works and relates to the world around it is crucial to address your productivity problem. Once the source of the problem is identified, you can find ways to improve yourself.

Third, you have to find **strategies to establish a productive mindset and lifestyle.** In this part of the book, you will learn actionable strategies, simple tricks, tips, and applicable methods to increase your productivity level. You will also learn how you could overcome the mental barriers you have unconsciously set up against your productivity. From over-analyzing to perfectionism, learning how to work around your quirks will help you achieve more out of your given time. One other important aspect you will develop with this book is finding balance in your life. Setting up boundaries between work, rest, and other pursuits is crucial to keeping yourself from getting overwhelmed. This part of the book will help you find that balance and maintain it.

Lastly, once you have adopted a productive lifestyle, the next step is to **find ways to sustain your productive**

lifestyle. Most probably, you cannot change overnight. From managing your time to avoiding distractions, this part of the book will help you sustain your changes and even build on the successes you have already achieved.

Now, all of this can be quite a lot to process. This is why I wrote this book in a manner that is easy to understand and, hopefully, engaging enough to get your imagination going. Please remember what you will learn here will be for nothing without acting. As such, every strategy, trick, and tip you will learn here is presented in a manner that is easy to apply. Now, with that out of the way, it is time that we go about turning you from a waiter to an active, productive go-getter.

Have fun!

CHAPTER I

THE PSYCHOLOGY BEHIND WHY WE PROCRASTINATE

"My evil genius Procrastination has whispered me to tarry 'til a more convenient season."

Mary Todd Lincoln

In the modern age, procrastination is putting things off until tomorrow and the day after (as the Greek poet Hesiod said almost 2800 years ago) and keeping ourselves busy doing unimportant tasks to avoid the important ones. As mentioned before, procrastination has existed since the time of ancient Egyptians and Greeks. New technologies such as the internet and social media have only created more procrastination opportunities.

Before anything else, it is essential to understand that procrastination is more than just about "being lazy". In fact, being a procrastinator does not have a lot to do with simple laziness. As a state of being, a procrastinator is remarkably self-aware. In essence, you know what you are doing is against your betterment, and the consequences of not finishing that task could be considerable. But, against your better judgment, you choose not to act or complete a task. To put it in even simpler terms: You know what you are doing is not good, but you do it anyway. This does give rise to the question: "Why do we procrastinate?".

Dealing with Negative Emotions

Can our mood affect our productivity? Psychology points to the affirmative with this question. Many of us know out of experience that we are less productive when we are in a bad mood. Procrastination is often a coping mechanism for the mind to handle certain moods. How this works is relatively simple. Suppose you were given a rather challenging task like, say, a 100-page report that needs to be done in a week. As soon as you receive the assignment, your brain starts to cycle through different emotions like apprehension, fear, and even annoyance.

In some cases, your brain is already creating future scenarios to get frustrated with the task. Overwhelmed by all of this negativity, your mind does what it thinks is the most sensible decision for that moment: put everything off until you are in a better mood. In essence, you won't even start to think about completing the task until you are in a better mental condition. In short, by procrastinating, your brain is doing some short-term mood repair and mental conditioning. In this instance, we can draw two possible sources for our procrastination.

A. The Task Itself

More often than not, we put off doing a task because we have attributed negative emotions to it. Simply put, we take so long to decide on doing something because we hate doing it in the first place. This cannot be avoided entirely as some tasks are downright dull and unpleasant by nature. Think about it, who enjoys checking income statements or cleaning dirty toilets? Even those who are good at them have only built a tolerance around these activities.

B. Personal Issues

In some instances, you put off tasks because of doubts or fears of failure or being misjudged. Perhaps you were going through a period of self-doubt and anxiety when that task was given to you. Here's a simple scenario: When you are about to start on that task, your mind suddenly starts thinking, "What do I do?" or "What will people think of this?" or "That's it, I'm not smart enough to finish this!". And so on. Whatever reason your brain suddenly came up with, the result is the same: you put down that task and do something else; most of the time, something more trivial.

In either case, procrastination intends to help our body and mind manage the stress and anxiety that comes with the task. However, the problem is that it is not doing a good job with it. Because it does nothing to alleviate the fact that you still have to do whatever you were assigned to perform. In most instances, your procrastination will only intensify the negative emotions you have with the task. Those feelings won't go away unless you complete what was asked of you.

The Irony of Procrastination

As was established a while ago, many people procrastinate to alleviate the negative emotions that come with specific tasks or situations. However, in reality, the opposite occurs. The longer we put off the intended task, the more pronounced our resentment will be about those situations.

Why is this so? Psychology points to a particular evolutionary trait we have acquired, which is called **Present Bias.** This is simply the tendency of an average human being to prioritize the short-term needs and concerns over long-term ones. Let's take a closer look at this Present Bias. When our ancient caveman ancestors moved out to the forest, and they heard two saber-tooth tigers nearby, which of the two beasts would you think they would have to deal with first? The one creeping in the bushes or the one a few hundred meters ahead looking over the cliffside? Logically, they would have to deal with the one closest to them. That's the one that has the highest chances of tearing them apart.

Here's a more relatable example. Suppose that you have $ 20 in your pocket right now for a haircut you intend to get a week from now. Suddenly, you feel hungry, and there's no food in the pantry. Would you save that $ 20 for that haircut, or would you use that to buy something from the nearest store? Probably, you will choose the latter.

For you, your future self is a stranger. His or her needs and concerns can be insignificant compared to your needs and concerns. You live in the present, after all. Your future self lives somewhere that has yet to exist. So, when we procrastinate, we are effectively putting that task off to be dealt with by our future selves. Your peace of mind now matters more than that version of you living a week from now. It is like deferring a problematic caller to another department. Here, that department is you living in the future.

What makes things worst is that our ability to make decisions that benefit us in the long-term tends to be impaired when we are placed under stress. Again, we point back to psychology for a reason.

Essentially, our brains have something called the Amygdala, a collection of cells near the base of the brain that detects and perceives outside threats. The only problem here is that the modern human brain, due to the lack of actual physical threats in their environment, will perceive uncomfortable tasks as "threats" to our well-being.

Even if our brain's logical part has carefully laid out an argument as to why we need to finish this task ASAP, the Amygdala screams and insists that that "threat" be removed from our very presence. And thus, in a spur of a moment, our brain finally decides to put off doing that task until the last minute.

The Intention and Action Gap

On the flip side, procrastination deals with time management just as much as it does with emotion regulation. In many cases, procrastination is a major symptom of a person's lack of or gradual decline of self-control. In essence, it happens when a person knows what they should do but cannot bring themselves to it. This is what psychologists call the Intention-Action Gap. This concept proposes that procrastination occurs because the person unconsciously lists all of their activities and categorizes them according to the amount of pleasure it gives them.

In practice, a procrastinator puts more value in the activities that give them immediate satisfaction at earlier times. As for important tasks, they are not ignored or given less weight. Instead, their order of priority is determined by how close they are to their deadline.

Here's a good example. Suppose you have specific tasks for an afternoon like cleaning the room, finishing a report, and mowing the lawn. You might also want to do certain activities like watching TV or playing a videogame somewhere in the afternoon. For an active person, the order of priority might be as follows:

A. Mow Lawn

B. Clean Room

C. Finish Report

D. Watch TV/Play Videogame

You could see that the person would put the task requiring the most focus and exertion and have a more significant impact first and relegate the less crucial activities last.

But for a chronic procrastinator, that order of priority could look something like this:

A. Watch TV

B. Play Videogame

C. ??????

D. ??????

E. Clean Room

F. ???????

G. ???????

H. Mow Lawn

I. ????????

J. ????????

K. Finish Report

Right from the get-go, you would notice that the list is poorly optimized. The tasks that give the most immediate satisfaction are done first while more pressing ones are put off last. In most cases, those important tasks will be done the next day.

Keep in mind that the gap only considers the time management aspect of procrastination. Even with a procrastinator, there is a certain level of guilt being felt when a more pressing task is put off for a later time. In essence, despite feeling relief that the uncomfortable task was being set aside, there is an overwhelming feeling of worry that what a procrastinator has just done might come back worse later. Procrastination covers both one's own mental preparations for a task as well as their valuation of the said task's importance. In essence, it is both a problem of regulating mood and managing time.

Neuropsychology of Procrastination

Today, many experts believe that procrastination is more than just how we perceive things or regulate our thoughts. In fact, it could have been hardwired into our very own psyche. Neuropsychology experts would point to procrastination as a deep-seated problem that affects the frontal lobes of the brain. This region of the brain governs all manners of executive functioning. And what is Executive Functioning, exactly? For the layman, it means merely all those functions that help you keep yourself organized. From solving problems to controlling your mood and even planning what needs to be done for a day or an hour, the frontal lobe functions by organizing all your thoughts to produce practical actions.

In essence, procrastinators are driven more by their brain regions that control mood and feelings than the more logical areas. A procrastinator evaluates tasks by how they feel about those tasks instead of their impact in the immediate future. Imagine that you have to study for a difficult exam the next morning. On the other hand, your roommate invites you to someone's birthday party a few blocks down. Typically, you would do a cost-benefit analysis of your options. If you go to the party, you might get to eat for free and meet people, but you miss out on your studying, and you might fail on that subject. If you choose to study, you increase your chances of passing that subject, but you might miss some good (and free) food and drinks and maybe some pleasant conversations. Essentially, one option is geared for long-term benefit, and the other for short-term advantage. For the procrastinator, every option is assessed based on their short term outcome. So, the choices will be made based on what they like to have NOW instead of what is required LATER.

In research done by the City University of New York, procrastination has been defined as an "inability to resist social temptations, immediate rewards, and pleasurable activities when the benefits of preparation are distant." It is also described as an "inability to use internal and external cues to determine when to initiate, maintain, and terminate goal-directed actions."

Now, those are rather complicated definitions for now. How does procrastination actually manifest? Here are some examples:

- Reduced agency (choosing options as if one has no control over them)
- Disorganization
- Poor emotion and impulse control

- Increased distractability
- Poor persistence in task
- Inability to sustain effort in long-term plans
- Deficiency in managing time and work

Why Do People Procrastinate?

Besides understanding why your brain is hardwired towards procrastinating, you also have to understand the defenses it sets up to legitimize your choices. After all, what's in mind won't hurt you until it starts dictating your every action.

When faced with a situation where we have to decide to act or not, we often gather whatever willpower we have to complete that task. At the best of times, we can even rely on our own goals to complete a task, especially if that goal involves some tangible reward. But the average human also inadvertently erects barriers against taking action or making decisions. As was stated, procrastination is a problem deeply rooted in the psyche that tends to outwardly manifest through our actions. But between that source and our actions are several nodes called reasons.

Here is the list of ten common reasons why people procrastinate. You might be surprised to find the ones that apply to your situation. Please remember to be as reflective and honest with yourself. Understanding the underlying reasons why you tend to procrastinate will eventually benefit you.

1. Your Goals Are Too Vague

The tendency to not do something is higher if the goal is not concrete. For example, you noticed that you are gaining weight and want to become healthier. So, you decide to put up the goal "Lose Weight" to be completed "As Soon as Possible". It's a good goal, right? Not really. Without specifics, you cannot make your goal actionable. What's the condition for victory in "Lose Weight"? Ten pounds at the end of the year? Or maybe more? Nobody knows, especially you. And what does a failure scenario look like? You gaining weight or remaining at that weight at the end of the year? Nobody knows, especially you.

2. The Rewards or Consequences are Too Long-Term

Procrastination often occurs when a person has to choose between short-term and long-term outcomes. What happens if that outcome is too far into the future? Most of the time, the mind would just discount it. Psychologists call this **Temporal Discounting**. If your boss tells you to prepare for an evaluation that happens in a month, you will most likely not act on it until a few days before the appointed date. Essentially, that time between you learning of that task and the time the outcome will occur will affect how much of a value you put in completing that task NOW.

3. No Regard for Your Future Self

Whether it be threats or rewards, the human mind tends to prioritize things with the highest chance of occurring very soon. This is what researchers call **Temporal Disjunction.** To make this exciting and simpler for you, think of yourself being divided into your present self and future self. If you have to choose whose needs have to be met, you'd instinctively choose your present. After all, the outcomes of the present determine the situations you will face in the future. However, temporal disjunction can also become a hindrance in decision-making. You might inadvertently think of your future self as a different person. So, you hand off the problem of completing a task to that person without considering what effects this might bring.

4. Focusing on Future Alternate Options

Suppose that you were to fix your roof as it is leaking rainwater in your kitchen. However, you decide to put off buying the necessary materials because you want to buy them at upcoming sale. While you wait for the sale, that hole in your roof just got bigger and bigger. Consequently, the expenses for the repairs just got more significant to the point that you buying the materials at lower prices didn't even matter.

Procrastinators tend to avoid acting to choose a better option in the future. They like to opt only for the best. The time it takes for that best option to arrive is not important. Although a bit of caution is healthy, taking too long to decide on something is a hindrance, especially in tasks with time constraints. In the end, you might not even follow through with your plan.

5. Optimism

More often than not, people procrastinate out of the sheer naivete that things are not as hard as they seem. You put off doing that task because you think you can do it in 3 days, not 7. You put off not going on a diet today because you can always do it tomorrow. And so on. The belief that tomorrow is the best day to do everything is a pitfall that many procrastinators fall in to. Every day will be tomorrow for your current frame of mind. So as long as you don't have to do it today out of the belief that things will be better tomorrow, you will keep putting the task off.

6. Indecisiveness

In some cases, the problem is not that you don't want to act. It is that you can't even decide which action to take in the first place. Indecision usually comes in two flavors: it's either not being able to decide between two options or the inability to decide as a part of a broader course of action. For example, you might want to lose weight but can't choose between Keto or Fasting. Another would be deciding to start a research paper but can't decide about the topic.

Usually, indecision is born out of a tendency to overthink what might happen if one course of action is taken over the others. This is called **Paralysis by Analysis.** Usually, there are three factors that an indecisive person tends to look upon in analyzing their options.

A. **Quantity** - The more options there are, the harder it is to make a choice.

B. **Diversity** - The more similar the options (concerning outcome or methodology), the harder it is to decide.

C. **Importance** - The more significant consequences or rewards a decision will generate, the harder it is to come to that decision.

Out of all the above reasons for procrastination, the last one takes a considerable amount of mental effort. After all, you will do significant mental gymnastics to justify why you can't come up with a conclusion. Hence, this reason is commonly called decisional procrastination. It is not that you don't want to act; you can't decide on how to act.

7. The Feeling of Being Overwhelmed

This reason is common in results-based environments like work or school. Suppose you were given an assignment that is both complicated and something that you have never done before. The feeling of being overwhelmed can come from the very nature of the task itself. Perhaps the task's scope is something you don't usually deal with, or maybe the task is a series of many smaller tasks that add up to each other. This sudden dump of information is going to be an assault on the brain. As such, the brain gets tired, trying to get a grasp of the situation. The mind just gets paralyzed, trying to understand the scope and magnitude of what needs to be done.

8. Impulsivity

Many procrastinators cannot complete specific tasks because they tend to act on a whim with little regard for the consequences of their actions. You might wonder what being impulsive has to do with procrastination. Isn't being impulsive just an erratic form of being active, which means it is far from what is considered as procrastinating? The answer is that the decision to procrastinate on a task is, in itself, based on impulse. When a procrastinator decides to put things off, their natural whims dictate their actions over the more logical and organized part of their brains. You understand that one action is of great importance, but you decide to do other activities instead, acting based on your primal urges.

9. The Search for Sensation

This is where the notion of "working well under pressure" comes into play. Some people are just hardwired to give 100% if there is a sense of pressure, excitement, and tension all around them.

For example, you choose to file your Income Tax Return on the date of the deadline because you are used to the rush of preparing the document and jsubmitting it in the last minutes. Doing it weeks earlier does not bring the same adrenaline rush that your mind is subconsciously looking for. This is called **Arousal Procrastination**, the act of putting things off until those activities give your body the sensations it desires. That rush can have the positive outcome of motivating a person to work at full capacity. However, this also leads to adverse outcomes such as rushing things through and low outcome quality. Getting used to this kind of dynamic can also be detrimental for you as it prevents you from working at your best without negative reinforcement.

10. Utter Dislike

More often than not, you just hate doing that task. Or perhaps you hate the person giving you the task or the general outcome that such a task brings. Either way, your resentment prevents you from getting the task done as soon as possible. In essence, your procrastination is some form of passive-aggressive rebellion against the powers beyond your control.

Understanding why and how our minds lean towards procrastination is the first step to find out how we might be able to limit our procrastinating tendencies. As discussed in this chapter, there are many reasons why we procrastinate. It would help a lot if you can find out what makes YOUR brain tick. The reasons mentioned above are just some of the more common factors for procrastination. In the next chapters, we will deal with more specific issues and how you could draw up a plan to overcome the roadblock that your mind and habits set up against you becoming a go-getter.

CHAPTER II

DISSECTING PROCRASTINATION IN DAILY LIFE

"Nothing is so exhausting as indecision, and nothing so futile."

Bertrand Russell

Now that you have understood how your brain can make you susceptible to procrastination, the next thing you have to deal with is this: What am I going to do now? Keep in mind that procrastination is a deep-seated problem in our minds. Addressing it should be done systematically, using strategies focused on various facets of our lives. It's going to be a long and sometimes arduous process. Hopefully, applying what you learn in this book will prove useful in this process.

In a nutshell, the process of addressing procrastination will involve two objectives:

1. Make yourself less uncomfortable with negative stimuli.

2. Care for more than just the present.

Sounds doable, right? That's because it is. But before we start with the process, let's take a closer look at how procrastination manifests in your life.

What Procrastination and Productivity Aren't

There is so much misinformation, myth, or downright lies about procrastination and productivity, which could hinder people from adopting a more productive lifestyle. As such, we should debunk some of these myths first.

Myth #1: Delay is Always Procrastination

This book does not support the notion that you should always leap into action without thinking about your decisions. Pausing or taking the time to reflect and weigh the prospects first is not necessarily procrastination. Although procrastinating is always delaying, but delaying is not always procrastinating. What's the difference here? To answer that question, realize that delay can always going to happen whether you like it or not. For example, you plan to take a flight to your holiday destination, but your flight is delayed because of bad weather conditions. You were not procrastinating, but you got delayed. It's out of your control.

What if you are an attorney tasked to represent a client at court, but the client lacks supporting evidence? Perhaps you would request the court for rescheduling of the trial. You are purposefully delaying, but you are doing so on reasonable grounds. However, if you want to mow your lawn but decide not to do it because you'd rather watch YouTube videos, you are procrastinating. In short, procrastination is delay done purposefully and irrationally.

Myth #2: It's in the Genes

If you are a slacker, does that mean that your kids are going to be slackers too? Or, the other way around, does that mean that you come from a long line of professional slackers? Scientific findings say no to these questions. Procrastination is highly dependent on the environment and the way we're raised. If a child is raised in an environment with a high level of dynamism and a strong push towards generating results, their chances of becoming chronic procrastinators are lower.

On the other hand, if a child grows up in a relatively undemanding environment, usually the opposite occurs. Either way, procrastination is not inherited, only enforced. The same applies to productivity.

Myth #3: It is All About Time Management

Procrastination due to poor time management is one of the more common myths since procrastination wastes time. However, that is actually a rather surface-level perspective. As mentioned in Chapter 1, procrastination is more than just a time management issue. People procrastinate due to many reasons, and most of them do not involve time. For example, many people fear failure and want things to work 100% at the first run. Others hate specific tasks, and some only care about what is more pleasant at the moment at the expense of postponing more important (but less enjoyable) tasks. Time is usually not an essential factor in dealing with procrastination, aside from sticking to a schedule.

Myth #4: Procrastination is the Same as Laziness

People often lump the two concepts together since they produce the same outcome: poor results or none at all. However, they are not the same. Laziness is defined as the state of idleness or unwillingness to devote time, effort, and energy to something. On the other hand, procrastination is the conscious pursuit of ineffectual and trivial goals instead of more important ones despite knowing the consequences.

Laziness is not working, while procrastination is about postponing essential things. Procrastination has a problem with prioritization. Laziness has a problem with commitment to doing things. However, they share the same motivators like aversion to work, rebellion against authority, and poor estimation of the task's nature. They are just different methodologies that lead to generally the same outcomes. With these myths sufficiently debunked, now is the time to go over the more observable procrastination aspects.

Mood Regulation

As mentioned before, procrastination is something that is deeply embedded in our minds. To be more specific about it, it's something that happens because of our mood. In theory, if you can make yourself feel less adverse towards a certain stimulus, you will be less likely to procrastinate. This is what psychologists call **Mood Regulation.**

Mood Regulation refers to a person's ability to control what they are feeling about a particular situation, idea, or stimulus in its more technical term. Simply put, it's those little defenses your mind has put up to make you feel at ease with something that you need to face head-on. "Wait," you say to yourself, "how do I regulate my mood? Is this something that I have to learn?". Technically, you don't have to learn how to regulate your mood. You can even do it by instinct.

Suppose you are given a complicated multi-phase project. Naturally, you would feel overwhelmed. But what did you do to cope with that emotion of being overwhelmed? Usually, people would take a brief walk to cool off. Others would be more passive-aggressive by blurting out a sarcastic remark like "tax returns again? My favorite!". Others take a quick smoke break. And others deal with the stress by venting it all out on others. Whatever the case, mood regulation is something that you can do by instinct. Also, what mood regulation strategy your brain chooses depends significantly on what mood you are feeling. To make this clearer, here are some examples.

A. Depression and Anxiety

When you experience low self-esteem and high stress levels, nearly every task you encounter will be unpleasant to you. As such, you'd rather lift your mood up first before you do anything. For example, you are feeling low levels of self-worth combined with a feeling of aversion towards the task you are given. Perhaps you think that the task is too challenging or that the person giving it is asking too much. Thus, you self-sabotage to prove that you were correct to feel this way. At the core of this emotion is what experts call **Emotional Dysregulation**. In essence, increasingly negative, low-energy emotions can impair the body's productivity levels to the point that the person cannot think straight or prioritize.

B. Anger

When one feels upset, your mind focuses on dealing with the anger first and will not resume any previous task until that anger is satiated. In other words, the mind emphasizes the emotion rather than what triggered that emotion. For example, you might be focusing on your studies when you suddenly got distracted by the noise coming from the neighbors. Maybe you go and ask the neighbors to keep it a bit quiet. Once you talked to the neighbors, do you immediately go back to your studies? Unless you have tremendous emotional stability, you won't. Instead, you'd take some time cooling yourself down before you resume studying. By that time, you might have already lost your train of thought and have to go a few steps back.

What makes anger particularly tricky is that its impulses tend to override all other thoughts just by its sheer intensity. As such, you'd be spending more time dealing with the fact that you are angry rather than what made you mad in the first place. However, there is a catch. At a certain level, anger becomes less of a cause for procrastination. This is because anger's contribution to task aversion can only go so far. If other distractions cannot change that mood, why bother pursuing such distractions? At this point of anger, the mind would instead focus on dealing with the task at hand while also letting the emotion run its course.

When We Fail to Regulate Our Emotions

As mentioned before, a common myth about procrastination is that it's because of laziness or poor time management. Of course, procrastination has something to do with time. In other words, procrastination becomes a problem once there are deadlines. However, it has been shown by many researchers (for example, Dr. Sirois and his colleagues at the University of Sheffield) that we procrastinate mainly because the intended task puts us in a lousy mood. By postponing that task, we try to repair our mood and let our future self handle the task. To find out why we procrastinate, we should first understand how our minds control our emotions.

Although everyone's situation is different, you'd be surprised to know that the brain follows roughly the same pattern when deciding to act or put things off. A great model to explain this process is proposed by the researchers at the Eindhoven University of Technology in The Netherlands.

This model uses the Cognitive Affective Processing System theory (or CAPS) to explain how many external and internal factors guide our minds to decide on whether to put off a task or not. CAPS is an important theory of personality. It was proposed by Walter Mischel and Yuichi Shoda in 1995 and explained how an individual's cognitive qualities (i.e., how our brains are wired) and the situational variable (i.e., the environment around us) would affect the development of our personality.

The Dutch researchers used an approach similar to that of CAPS to consider internal and external factors to explain our brain's procrastination process. The internal factors in this model are avoidance and impulsiveness, and the external factors are related to the environment and the task itself.

Let's take a closer look at each of these factors:

- Avoidance occurs because we perceive the task as threatening or unattractive. Hence, we procrastinate to avoid pain.

- Impulsiveness is choosing short-term benefits over long-term costs; in other words, the inability to delay gratification.

- The situational factor of the environment (whether at work or in personal life) could significantly impact procrastination. For example, suppose the consequences of missing an important deadline at work or the penalty for a bill's late payment is big enough. In that case, we might bring our procrastinating tendencies under control.

- The task itself could be annoying, dull, or challenging. All of these contribute to higher chances of procrastination.

One tends to procrastinate due to the perceived anxiety he or she gets from performing a task. This anxiety could be anchored on how you perceive yourself or drawn from your experiences. It could even be from your misconceptions about specific tasks. Regardless of what perceived anxiety we have, such emotion leads us to pursue other pleasurable activities to "brighten our mood." After all, why go through all that unpleasant emotion when you can choose something more uplifting to your mood?

Motivation (and De-Motivation)

Remember that procrastinators know the consequences of putting things off until the last moment. The fact that such consequences exist can be a source of stress and anxiety, too. This stress and anxiety could sometimes cause even more procrastination. In other words, while we procrastinate to get short-term relief, we also experience tension and uneasiness because we are still worried about our decision's consequences.

So, how could we experience relief and stress at the same time? This is what psychologists call Cognitive Dissonance, where the brain can analyze and prepare for different sets of mental problems at the same time while also guiding the body's essential locomotive functions.

How cognitive dissonance works is rather ingenious. Let us say that you choose to put off preparing an important presentation until later in the afternoon so that you can first complete a few easier and less essential tasks. In the first few minutes of your procrastinating, your brain could send out little reminders like "Hey, about that presentation. You should do it ASAP!" while also subconsciously introducing tension in your body. A couple of hours later, that voice becomes louder and commanding like "Presentation. Now!" while that feeling of uneasiness increases in your body. Finally, you relent, prepare the presentation, and get relieved. In essence, you chose to relax because you feel stressed with the task. But choosing to relax made you even more stressed out. It was only in the completion of the task that you finally experienced some form of release. This cycle generates a form of negative reinforcement. Your brain is subconsciously injecting the body with stress to seek relief by getting the task done. The catch here is that the dissonance must happen at the right time to foster mental health. What if you are in a situation where rest is required, but that little voice in your head is giving out all sorts of thoughts to keep you awake at night?

The problem with many procrastinators is that the voice finally kicks them into action when it's too late. It's at that point late at night when the body is supposed to sleep that the brain finally tells you, "hey, you should have done more today." That reminder is a bit too late now and robs the body of its required rest time. In turn, your body will not be in the best condition to be productive the next day. It's a self-defeating behavior that feeds on itself and becomes more and more acute when procrastination becomes chronic.

Meeting Your Future Self

As of now, there is still one person you have yet to meet and whose needs and concerns you often do not consider in your decisions. That person is, well… you. Or, to be more specific, that version of you who has yet to exist. Your Future Self.

More often than not, the future self takes the back seat as far as our decisions are concerned. Whatever our choices are, they always seem to serve our present selves. This problem is not exclusive to procrastinators. Nearly everyone decides to prefer their present self over the future one. But that does beg the question: if the current version of you has the means to solve a problem, why give it to your future self?

To illustrate this, here's a scenario. Suppose that you have $20.00 on your hand now. You have the option to spend that on something nice like, say, dinner at Red Lobster or to save it. Typically, you'd go for a fancy dinner since that will satisfy your current need. Any money-related problem you might encounter in the future, and where that $20.00 can come in handy, is something that your future self will have to deal with.

This apparent disconnect between our current and future selves is one of the most significant contributors to procrastination. Think of it as you and your future self being two separate, competing teams. When a problem is lodged at the "Now" Department, the team's procrastinating members decide to defer the issue to the "Future" Department since the former believes the latter has better means of solving it.

Thus, if being disconnected from your future self contributes towards procrastination, then the opposite would prevent it, right? Most probably, yes! Ask yourself how your choice will affect you in the future. If you, choose to do things now, you have more free time later on. So, instead of your future self having to deal with the task, they could relax, have more free time, do other stuff, etc.

Time-Wasters: What Contributes to Our Procrastination?

So far, we've been talking about mostly internal factors that contribute to procrastination and lack of productivity. However, that is just a part of the story. Whether we are at home or work, the very things surrounding us can ultimately impede us from achieving something for that day. So what exactly contributes towards us procrastinating on our tasks?

One Important Note: Do remember that these are not negative factors. You can't completely do away with them. This is to help you consider adjusting your choices in light of their presence in your life. Here are some of the main contributors to our procrastination:

1. Family members

This is quite common when you are at home or working from home. For example, your children demand constant attention, which creates a distraction and sometimes stress. If you are trying to fix your roof but, suddenly, little Timmy's box fort just collapsed in the backyard, you have to pick up after them. Or what if you are in the middle of filing a report but have to run errands for your wife, pacify fighting kids, or clean after the mess made by the family pet? In essence, interactions with family members add multiple side-activities that are distracting.

2. Your Email

Do not get the wrong idea. Checking your email is a rather important activity. After all, there is information you need to know or act upon as soon as possible. Things like reminders of upcoming payments and announcements from your family, work, and friends are information that you need to know ASAP. All of those emails become a problem if you don't have a system to process them efficiently. What if you suddenly got 100 emails for that day? You could spend hours reading and answering them all. The essential point to keep in mind here is to prioritize your tasks. For example, if there are more critical tasks, skim through the emails and only read and reply to the highest priority ones and leave the rest for later.

3. Your Gadgets

A direct result of our immersion in technology is that we become dependent on them, and our connections can reach us at any moment. For example, you might instinctively reach out for your phone from time to time just to check out what's happening with your friends on Facebook or to reply to their messages. Gadgets like smartphones, tablets, and gaming consoles could easily distract us and provide excellent procrastinating opportunities.

4. Noise

What constitutes noise could be different from one person to another. Some could tolerate a few unwelcome sounds, and others must have full control of ambient sounds to keep focus. Either way, noise is any sound that interrupts your train of thought. This audio distraction could be coming from the people around you; colleagues at work or noisy kids at home, or the streets outside your office or home. All of these could prevent us from getting started, especially if the tasks at hand are challenging or require concentration.

5. Other Tasks

Besides your schedule, there will be other tasks you have to deal with in your work area. Suppose your boss suddenly wants you to give him a project update while working on another document? What if your co-workers want you to help them with something? And so on. It could even be problems that suddenly sprang up. One good example of this is equipment malfunctions. The printer is going haywire, the TV's signal is busted, the operating system on your laptop requires an update and a restart, etc. Since these are unavoidable, you are tempted to finish them first, which takes time off your initial task.

Taking Control

Fortunately, there is a lot you can do to reduce the chances of procrastinating. This will involve dealing with the internal and external factors discussed before. Here are some tips on managing these internal and external factors.

A. Dealing with Your Mood

As mentioned before, we procrastinate mainly because the intended task puts us in a lousy mood. Hence, learning to regulate our mood better is essential. We all know it isn't easy to always be in a good mood. That's why our goal here is to "regulate" our mood in such a way that the negative emotions do not last for very long and hence, do not drag us into excessive procrastination.

1. Reduce Perceived Anxieties

When we consider a task challenging, or we're afraid that the outcome will not be good enough, we will perceive anxiety. Our minds will try to relieve us by postponing that task. Finding the root cause of this anxiety could make it easier to face that task. For example, if you feel overwhelmed by a task because it's quite big, like a thesis, you can break the task down into smaller sub-tasks and focus on completing those sub-tasks. The point here is to turn that one massive task into smaller, manageable ones. This should reduce your apprehension about the task while increasing your belief in finishing the entire project on time.

2. "Draw Closer"

You could use one other solution to close the distance gap between you and the averted task while increasing the distance between you and procrastination. You can make the task more convenient. For example, if you tend to procrastinate on paying your monthly bills because you hate lines, dealing with people at a counter, or receiving bills regularly, you can make the payment online or set-up automatic payments. So as long as you can perform the task without having to deal with the anxiety-causing factor, then you are good to go.

3. Stabilize Your Sleeping Patterns

You can plan for your next day in advance. Briefly reviewing the plans for tomorrow before you go to sleep will allow your brain to get ready for the upcoming tasks. Focusing on what to do tomorrow could prevent you from beating yourself up on what you failed to do today.

Developing a habit of planning in advance, could reduce the lack of direction you might feel as you wake up and the emotional dysregulation that prevents you from getting "into the mood" for work. To make the planning as effective as possible, you need to combine it with dealing with your anxieties, as discussed in the previous section. Otherwise, you might still have to deal with the negative emotions you have attributed to a task before you sleep. And remember, negative emotions can disturb your sleeping!

4. Prepare Your Emotions for Work

At the start of the day, review your to-do list for that day. to psyche yourself up for the tasks ahead. A prepared mind can handle the tasks more comfortably. This will help the mood-regulating regions of the brain organize the emotions it must allow manifesting for the person to work properly. The goal here is to let the emotions that help you perform at optimum levels rise to the surface. Think of it like jump-starting a car engine, but the engine in this situation is your mood.

At the same time, you can determine what emotions you tend to display when you're working efficiently. Perhaps you work best with emotions like joy or better with something stable like a calm focus. Whatever the case, you should reflect on what moods are the most compatible with your work and help them surface before starting the day.

5. Analyze and Reduce

Going back to the CAPS structure, perhaps the best strategy you could use is to reduce the factors that cause anxiety in the first place. This is called Inquiry-Based Stress Reduction or IBSR. This process involves three steps. First, lay out all the procrastinatory conditions and group them according to emotions, effects, causes, short-term benefits, and consequences. For example, if you are tasked with finishing an assignment. Perhaps your procrastinatory conditions are as follows:

- Emotion: Anxiety
- Cause: Bad experience with a similar task before
- Short-Term Benefit: Improved mood
- Consequence: A lousy grade.

Next, imagine another reality where these procrastinatory conditions are absent from your mind, and the context behind the task is different. This should make it easier for you to adopt a new perspective regarding the task. For example, the anxiety caused by the size of the task could be reduced by dividing the task into smaller sub-tasks. After completing one or more of the subtasks, confidence will replace the anxiety, and you could start imagining the opposites for each procrastinatory condition. In the example above, this could look like the following:

- **Emotion:** Confidence
- **Cause:** Success with a similar task previously completed
- **Short-Term Benefit:** Reduced hesitation and anxiety
- **Consequence:** A good grade.

B. Dealing with Noise

Once you have dealt with the introspection above, you can start making things around you work to your advantage. Here are four strategies that you can use.

1. Get People Around You on Board

If you need to concentrate at work or be left alone for a while at home, you have to inform the people around you. This is especially important for working from home. Inform your family members about your work schedule and convince them not to disturb you for the most critical hours. You can even set up a signaling system that helps those around you know whether or not it is now okay to interrupt you with something. Something as easy as a "Do Not Disturb" sign at your door should be good enough.

2. Set Priorities for Your Daily Communications

Nowadays, we engage in various communication types, for example, Emails, messages on different social media platforms, phone calls, video calls, etc. Reading through all that email backlog and answering those messages can take a lot of time. This is not only a productivity-killer but also an excellent opportunity to procrastinate. We cannot get rid of communications altogether. However, we can set priorities. For example, we can start the day by skimming through the emails and messages, decide which ones need our immediate attention, and leave the rest to a later time.

You can also devote a specific time of the day just to reading emails. This should not be longer than, for example, half an hour. Choosing when to allocate this half of an hour is up to you. When you need to focus on your computer screen or read a report or finish any other task, turn off the TV, and put your cellphone aside. You are the best person to decide on when to access social media during working hours. If done excessively, social media could provide ample procrastinating opportunities.

3. Organize Your Work Space

For many people, clutter can also be a form of psychological noise. To avoid this, de-clutter and organize your workspace (or your home office).

Dedicate one area to documents, another for the laptop, a corner for the notes, and so on. Place everything within reach. This will reduce the chances of you fumbling through your desk for specific items, preventing you from breaking your focus.

4. Stick to the Plan

Now, all of these systems and plans would be for nothing if you cannot commit to them. Consciously and regularly organize your workspace and routines. This will allow your brain to value those routines, and it will do its best to remember them and commit to the plan. Most of what we discussed in this section applies to workplaces or working from home. But they could be used to getting any task requiring focus and structure done.

And when you complete a task under these systems, do allow yourself to take a rest. This will help your brain correlate the systems with the benefits of sustaining your efforts on a long-term basis.

To summarize:

There is no way for you to remove altogether the factors that lead to procrastination. They will always lurk in your brain or in your surroundings, waiting for the right moment to pop up and make you hesitate.

However, it is better to show effort in addressing procrastination and reduce its effects than doing nothing at all. It will take some time and practice before you get the hang of it, but you should identify the causes of procrastination as they occur. Once identified, all that is left to do is prevent them from impacting your productivity. In the next chapter, we will talk about our habits and how they could be friends or foes to our productivity.

CHAPTER III

OUR UNPRODUCTIVE HABITS

"The time to begin most things is ten years ago."

                              Mignon McLaughlin

So far, we've only been talking about our mind's inner workings and the external factors that contribute to procrastinating. Now, the question you may ask is:

How do You become Unproductive?

Unproductiveness involves more than the mental processes as laid out in the previous chapter. In most cases, procrastination is the starting point of being unproductive; it delays when we get started with a task, reduces the amount of time available to finish the task and, usually reduces the output quality.

To get the desired result with any task, we need two ingredients:

- Getting started; this is where procrastination comes into the picture.

- Completing the task within the available time and with acceptable quality; here is where productivity matters.

Hence, while procrastination and productivity are not the same, they are closely related as they are the ingredients of completing any intended task.

Everyone procrastinates from time to time, and we all know it's impossible to be always productive. However, sometimes we develop specific behavior patterns that regularly push us to procrastinate or have very low productivity. These habits are far beyond one instance of inactivity or unproductivity and are more like instinctive responses.

The Faces of Procrastination and Unproductiveness

As discussed in the previous chapter, the internal and external factors contributing to procrastination will differ from one person to another. Similarly, the way procrastination manifests itself could vary per person. Nevertheless, most of our procrastination can fall under a handful of categories. In fact, you can group them in four primary "Flavors" as we will discuss shortly. Each of these flavors is like a behavior pattern or habit. It delays the starting point of a task and can end up in low output quality. Hence, these habits could become manifestations of both procrastination and unproductivity.

A. The "I Work Well Under Pressure" Guy

These procrastinators live that David Bowie and Freddie Mercury Duet to the letter by living off the rush from doing things in a hurry. For these people, nothing is worth doing without excitement. And what is more exciting than a good old-fashioned time limit? When Under Pressure Procrastinators receive a task that needs to be done in two weeks, they will start working on it the last week before the deadline. If they really want a premium rush, they'd do it the day before the deadline. There are two schools of thought as to why this type exists. First, there is that need for perfection in the task. If the task has a time limit, the mind works at 100%, so the chances of sound output are relatively high, or at least in theory.

The other reason is in the belief in the "11th Hour Save", i.e., waiting until the latest possible time before it's too late. There is this notion that every force in the universe will conspire and work in tandem when the stakes are high for a person. Whether or not that is true is best left to philosophers and quantum physicists to discuss.

Whatever the case, this kind of procrastination sacrifices preparation and risks the output quality and meticulousness. It assumes that eventually, the task could be done with speed and optimum performance. In most cases, this approach is not sustainable.

B. The Self-Deprecator

This kind of procrastinator is given birth for reasons that are not precisely of our own doing. The self-deprecators are usually productive people and can take on task after task. However, they do tend to overwork themselves to the point that they blame themselves for moments of inaction. For example, imagine someone who has completed several reports for that day receives one more assignment. Tired from his previous tasks and frustrated at the new one just given to him, he raises his hand and exclaims, "eh, whatever. I'll do this tomorrow because I'm feeling sluggish right now!"

People showing this behavior are tired of the constant stress and pressure. This type usually happens among men where there is an intense fear of admitting one's tiredness. The self-deprecator is essentially a person at the wrong place at the wrong time. The lack of rest keeps them from performing at optimum levels to the point that they start slacking off later tasks. To put it in simpler terms, they just really need a big break to rest and relax.

C. The Busybody

Do not get the wrong idea. Doing a lot of things is a sign of a productive person. After all, how else could you be trusted in doing a lot of tasks if you have not proven that you can carry such a workload? However, this becomes a problem if the busyness becomes an excuse for why you don't get things done. For instance, if you have nine tasks to do that day but fail to do the last three, the most likely reason you will blurt out is "I was busy!". This is one of the more passive-aggressive manifestations of Task Aversion.   Instead of admitting that you don't like to do something, you'd rather hide behind your busy work schedule. That way, you hope that the task gets shuffled to another person.

D. The Easily Distracted

This type of procrastinator suffers from a terminal disease called The Dangling Keys Syndrome. If something gets their attention, you could bet that their sole focus is on that thing now instead of what they were previously working on. Here's how this works: suppose that you are about to fill up your income tax return form. That should take you about an hour or two to complete. However, you find out that your best pen's cover is missing, and you can't start on the task until you have that cover found. So, you go about spending an hour dismantling your room to find the pen cover and then go back to your task of filling up the ITR form.

The problem with this kind of procrastinator is their inability to follow things through. They are good at getting things started but can quickly drop them when something new bothers them. This inconsistency and frequent shifts of effort can lead to burnout because this procrastinator takes on many tasks but cannot finish any of them.

E. The Perfectionist

This procrastinator works with ideals. To them, nothing is worth doing until the best conditions are set up. For them, everything has to be in perfect order (even their mood) before they start doing anything. This type of procrastinator is fixated on the idea of perfection.

Everything has to be done either their way 100% or not done at all. Consequently, this procrastinator has a strong imagination but a considerable inability to execute that same imagination. This tendency has some roots in fear of failure. So as long as that perfect idea remains, well, an idea, then it can't be attacked or proven wrong. It's better to have a perfect idea than a half-baked plan, or so as this type of procrastinator thinks.

F. The Avoider

Whereas the Busybody hides behind their schedules to avoid the task, the avoider just, for the lack of a better term, avoids. Where the busybody says, "I'm busy. Don't bother me!", the avoider raises his hand in defeat and does not think about the task anymore. The reasons why the avoider procrastinates is several. First, there is an aversion to the task itself. Perhaps you have some negative experience doing tasks of similar nature. Alternatively, you hate the person giving you the task in the first place. Another reason is the fear of failure. You don't like making mistakes, and mistakes do tend to appear less if you work less. Lastly, there is the fact that you just feel overwhelmed by your task. Perhaps the task is too complicated or challenging. In any of these cases, you'd rather not think about completing the task regardless of the consequences of putting it off.

G. The Over-Analyzer

This procrastinator is actually doing a lot of work. The only problem is that that work is done only in their mind. This procrastinator sets up charts and diagrams in their brain. However, those diagrams are focused too much on what *might* happen instead of *making things happen*.

An example of this is when you are going to prepare the results of a project for your teammates. As you think of the different ways to do the presentation, you start thinking of the possible adverse outcomes of any route you take. If you choose route A, then consequences 1, 2, 3, 4, and 5 might happen. If you select route B, then outcomes 6, 7, 8, and 9 might happen. And so on.

The problem with this kind of procrastination is that it is the right amount of effort being exerted in the wrong channel. Being mindful of what each decision brings, good or bad, is necessary. But if you subject yourself to Paralysis by Analysis, you are not doing much to complete your task anyway.

H. The "Bitten More Than He Could Chew" Guy

This procrastinator seems like a victim of their circumstances. Perhaps you are given a new task that you have absolutely no experience with before, or you are required to go somewhere new. It's not that you don't want to do the task, but you find yourself way in over your head for it.

For this procrastinator, there are three main problems:

- **Time:** "What, I only got that long to do all of this?"

- **Contacts:** "Who's going to help me? Where should I go? Who should I ask advice for?"

- **Knowledge**: "But I don't know how to do THAT! Where do I start? What resources do I need? How am I going to do this if even I don't know what I'm looking at?!"

This procrastinator tends to find problems rather than opportunities for solutions. The procrastinator of this type opines the mere fact that he is utterly resource-less compared to the task. As such, they can spend a whole lot of time bellyaching before they could even decide to think about starting the task.

Which of these Procrastinators Are You?

You need to realize that you might belong to more than one of the types mentioned above. You may procrastinate in one way for one instance and another in a separate incident. You may even fall in between two groups at the same time.

Whatever the case, each person has their reasons and motivations for procrastinating. Whether it is out of fear of failure, a desire to be as perfect as possible, or even the need to get a rise out of doing things in a hurry, there is no such thing as procrastination for procrastination's sake.

The Psychology of Productivity

Until now, we have been talking about different habits of procrastination and unproductiveness. But what about the opposite? How can a person embrace productivity? To answer that question, you have to realize that learning about productivity is also about learning what works for you and not just how you set yourself up for failure. The concept of being productive is rather broad. However, that does not mean that you cannot anchor yourself on some facts to embrace a more productive lifestyle.

A. The Limits of the Will

Talking about willpower seems a little bit outdated these days. With all the developments and new ideas, everybody who thinks they know about productivity would talk about things like your "ego", "mood", and "perspective". But as outdated as the concept of willpower is, it is the one that directly affects your productivity. The reason for this is because will, in contrast to the brain's seemingly infinite calculating potential, is a finite resource. How well you use this limited resource dramatically impacts your productivity.

Suppose you are required to finish an exam in a room filled with music blaring at full volume. The chances are that you are not going to finish that paper. Why is this so? It's because two things are depleting your willpower simultaneously: the task of completing the exam and the task of maintaining focus without getting distracted by the music.

Everyone has a finite amount of willpower every day. A portion of that willpower gets used every time you decide on something or, in some cases, exert maximum focus. This is why you often feel indecisive at 6 pm when you have spent the whole day working. Your willpower at that time is considerably spent along with your body's strength. Marketers have taken advantage of this depletion of willpower by bombarding you with many advertisements during the "prime time" periods starting from 6 to 10 in the evening. With your will gone, you are more susceptible to subliminal messaging.

B. Every Decision Uses Willpower

Decision-making, by design, is a mentally taxing activity. Decisions can be made in a split-second in the brain, but there is actually a lot going on inside your head in those tiny seconds. You weigh options, predict outcomes, and go through many details. Processing that sheer amount of data within that short period is going to expend a lot of your willpower.

To demonstrate how this consumption of willpower occurs in a typical day, let's go through one day and review various decisions we might need to make. At the day start, you should decide on the clothes you wear, the breakfast you prepare, what to take for lunch for yourself and maybe for the kids, etc. As the day goes, you use more brainpower in complex tasks like finishing reports, negotiating with clients, and dealing with problems, and so on. At the end of the day, your choices tend to get simpler. Perhaps you'd settle for fast food for dinner or grab the nearest shirt without consideration of its type or color. This is because you are considerably spent at that moment and do not want to make more complex thinking.

This is why more productive people make schedules for their day. In this way, they don't have to use up a lot of their willpower for every decision they make. By regimenting your life, you can effectively cut off your mind's consumption of willpower. Thus, you tend to make better decisions all day long. (More of this will be discussed later on in the following chapters).

C. Multitasking: Why It Isn't Real

If the brain consumes a finite amount of willpower for every decision, would it make sense to just multi-task?

That way, you can do two things at once and make your brain think that it is only doing one thing. The answer is no. Multi-tasking, as we understand it, is a misnomer. The brain is designed to focus on one item of attention at any given moment. If you file your taxes now, it will focus on that ITR form in front of you. If you choose to clean your kitchen, your brain focuses on removing that dirt from the tabletop. Never can your mind focus on the two items of attention at any single given instance. The brain goes through two stages when shifting between tasks:

A. **Goal Shifting** - It changes the focus of its attention.

B. **Rule Activation** - It establishes the parameters for what needs to be done in that instance.

Now, shifting between tasks takes up a considerable portion of your willpower. Imagine doing that shift hundreds of times within a short time. At the end of that period, you would have spent your day's supply of willpower, which leaves you mentally weakened for the rest of the day. This is what researchers call **Switching Cost,** where the constant shifting of tasks and focuses negatively affects a person's cognitive functions.

Yes, some people are known to successfully multi-task in its most real sense, but they are more of the exception than the norm. For the rest of the ordinary people, the "one item to focus per moment" rule is in effect.

Otherwise, you are more likely to lose focus and fail on your tasks.

How to Know If you are a Chronic Procrastinator?

So, how would you know that you have developed a tendency towards chronic procrastinating? In other words, how do you know that you are in the 20% chronic procrastinators (as mentioned in the introduction)? Fortunately, it is easy to tell if you have created a procrastinating habit as long as you have a decent amount of self-awareness. Just keep in mind that there is a considerable difference between sporadic procrastination and chronic ones. With that out of the way, be mindful of the following symptoms.

A. General Aimlessness

Simply put, you feel utterly aimless and spent once a project is completed. With that rush gone and all of your willpower poured into completing the task at a hectic pace, your ability to work at optimum levels is no longer there. As such, you take quite a lot of time before you embark on a new project, which can make you a liability in time-oriented environments. When you do accept a new task, you won't know where to start. The magnitude of the task at hand could be overwhelming to your perspective. As such, you instinctively put completing the task off until the last minute.

B. Lack of Timeliness

Punctuality is one of the first casualties once you develop a procrastinating habit. This is because you now tend to underestimate the amount of time needed to finish the task. As such, you miss out on arriving on time for important meetings and get started with tasks on time.

C. A Never-ending Task List

That timetable you spent hours organizing does not seem to get finished. More tasks are added while existing ones remain unchecked and unfinished. There is no doubt that you are busy, but you cannot accomplish anything within the foreseeable future.

D. Focusing on Trivial Stuff

Perhaps the worst of the symptoms, this one prevents you from focusing on a critical task at a time. You will find your train of thought being broken by smaller, less-important tasks. For example, you might find yourself filing a report but suddenly shift to arranging the books on your desk because you noticed one item out of place. Or you could be hosting a party at home but focus on fixing the look of your sofa instead of welcoming guests.

What makes it worse is that such needless shifting of tasks gives the sensation of being busy. Although that is technically true, but you are not buy with the right things. The advent of social media and handheld technology has allowed individuals several distractions waiting to be given attention in their pockets. Browsing the internet for useless trivia or checking in on your friends' lives is one of the most significant sources of unproductivity in the office.

Do all of these symptoms need to show for you to realize that you have become a chronic procrastinator? Not really. One should be enough that you are developing a preference for putting important tasks over trivial things.

To summarize:

Everyone procrastinates from time to time; there is always something more interesting than what we need to do at this moment. In this chapter, we discussed various types of avoidance archetypes and reviewed their procrastinating habits. Figuring out which type you belong to could provide a better understating of why you procrastinate and help with limiting or hopefully eliminating your procrastinating tendencies. Once you know more about how you set yourself up for procrastination with your decisions and actions, you can start addressing your procrastinating habits, one quirk at a time.

CHAPTER IV

BUSY, BUT NOT PRODUCTIVE

"It is not enough to be busy; so are the ants. The question is: What are we busy about?"

Henry David Thoreau

Wouldn't it be great to get more done consistently? The ability to do a lot within a set limit of time is something that many people strive for (and many employers look for). But you might be wondering, "what if I'm already busy?". Let me stop you there. What you should be aiming for is not to be busy but to be productive. How big is the difference between being busy and being productive? Well, it's enormous!

Why Being Busy is Not Ideal

More often than not, you may have measured how productive your day is by how busy or hectic it was. That constant movement often gives us the feeling that we are needed, influential, and doing something that contributes to our long-term success.

Do you think having a full schedule for a day equals a sizeable output for that day? Sometimes it does, but most of the time it doesn't! Real productivity comes from deliberately spending our time on things that matter, not cramming too many things to be done within a single hour. In fact, being unnecessarily busy can impede you in several ways. Here are four examples:

1. No More Self-Reflection

Being in a constant state of motion makes it hard for you to do some course correction when necessary. By focusing more on being "active" than accomplishing what matters, you rob yourself of the time needed to stop and think if what you are doing is contributing to your long-term goal. This goes back to how finite our mental energies are. If you use them up carelessly and without prioritization, you won't have much left to do some introspection. It's necessary to ask yourself now and then, "hey, am I still in the right direction?" or "Is it time to make a change?" or "Maybe I should take a vacation". With your mental energy spent for that day from tackling too many things, you'll most likely spend your free time just recuperating and preparing for another hectic round.

2. False Sense of Accomplishment

So, you have set up several tasks that need to be completed for that day, and, by sheer perseverance on your part, you managed to check every item off. It feels good, right? Once you have dealt with the stress, your body releases hormones to relax. This is where that "feel good" sensation comes after you have managed to survive a hectic day. But, again, what matters is the impact that those tasks make. Did they really matter or not? Accomplishing many tasks for a day and feeling good about it only works if those tasks contribute to achieving a bigger goal. If not, then you might have been wasting precious time on trivial pursuits.

3. Excuses

Most of the time, you will not complete every task for a day, depending on how packed your schedule is. As such, our busyness can be an easy excuse for why we can't finish every task in our day. In fact, you could use your busyness as an excuse as to why you'd rather not do something that you are uncomfortable with or confront a seemingly unpleasant situation. Remaining busy (at least on the surface!) can provide you with the opportunity to avoid whatever you don't like. Your boss gives you an assignment that you don't like? Show them your loaded schedule and ask them to give it to someone else. You need to go to the doctor but dread what disease they might discover in you? Just tell the doctor that you have an important meeting that day. And so on. If you find yourself using your busyness as an excuse not to get the right things done, you are sabotaging your productivity.

4. The Death of Creativity

Although you may have grown up, you are still required to let your mind play from time to time. One of the best ways to entertain yourself is to do something creative. It's a form of stress relief as well as mood regulation.

But if your day is too packed, you limit your time and energy to get creative. When everything in your day is measured and time-tabled, you will spend your mental energies on dealing with all those tasks. You won't have enough if you encounter a situation where you have to think outside the box. This is why a bit of slack time is needed between tasks. Being busy all the time consumes your time and energy. Your mind won't be able to unload some of the burdens it had picked up, and to replenish itself. If you hop from one task to another for the whole duration of the working day, you prevent your creative side from rising to the surface.

Busyness vs. Productivity

Let's get this out of the way, what makes productivity different from busyness? Nowadays, these two terms are often mixed up. Some would even think that having clogged up work schedules and tons of unfinished paperwork mean that you are going somewhere in life. This could not be farther from the truth.

Being busy is hectic while being productive is organized and focused. Being busy is being in constant action while being productive is having an impactful output. Being busy is endless multi-tasking while being productive is working deeper and getting more critical tasks done. Busy people are owned by their crammed schedule, while productive people are the owners of their agenda.

Here are six ways how being productive is different from being busy:

1. Busy People Work Hard; Productive People Work Smart

Busy people are often hard-workers. Their ability to stick to a schedule and work in a system gives them motivation. But just because you work hard and try to function with a system does not mean you will achieve the most. On the other hand, productive people are more focused on efficiency, i.e., finding better ways to do things. Yes, there is still that system and schedule in place, but a productive person finds opportunities to optimize such structures.

Each group operates on different philosophies. Busy People focus more on doing all much as possible. But productive people focus more on being effective. They can understand how to optimize the process by removing redundant tasks and streamlining the flow of work. Here's an example. If the workspace generates a lot of trash, the least that a busy person can do is stick to a workspace cleanup schedule. On the other hand, a productive person puts up waste bins for different trash, disposes of unwanted materials when he makes them, and avoids extensive cleaning at regular intervals.

2. Busy People Get Lost in the Details. Productive People Focus on Details That Matter.

A busy person knows what makes detail A, B, C, D, and E different from each other. However, they also end up wasting too much time trying to reconcile the differences and flaws between such options. On the other hand, productive people can focus only on details with a big impact on the end result. In other words, they pay attention to details without losing sight of the bigger picture. They can find ways to meet the needs of the broader goals while also addressing more minor ones.

Focusing on details that matter the most is a core principle of the 80/20 rule, which will be discussed in more detail later. Of course, being mindful of the details is crucial. Stanley Kubrick infamously had that scene where Shelley Duvall is warding off Jack Nicholson with a baseball bat in The Shining shot 127 times because he did not like some small details (including Duvall's phoned-in acting). But the end result was a more realistic scene where you could feel the terror and frustration in Duvall's character.

What is essential to understand is the overall impact of that detail, regardless of its size and scope. A productive person focuses on things that will contribute to the meeting of an overall goal. As for the rest, they find ways to delegate, improvise, eliminate, and optimize.

3. Productive People Are Capable of Saying "No".

The ability to check off items in your to-do list is a good thing. But even better is if you can decide what to do and when to do them. The truth is that busy people act as if they are incapable of saying No to any request or task. There is that occasional side-task here, that favor from a co-worker there, and that mini-project a few days later.

Productive people, on the other hand, can respectfully decline in certain situations. They understand that every "yes" they give will consume their time later on, and too many of these responses will eventually set them up for failure in the future. By learning how to say "No", a productive person protects the one valuable source that is limited for everyone: time.

4. Busy People Do It Solo. Productive People Delegate.

Now, there is nothing wrong with doing things by yourself if you can do it. Tons of projects can be done alone, provided that you have the skills and time management necessary to assume different roles. However, what is wrong is if you insist on doing things on your own when there is a readily available option to have others help you on your task. A productive person understands this and, as such, invests in letting others assist him with his task. Sure, he might have to do some favors for them in return, but this does not remove the fact that the productive person takes off a considerable chunk of his workload by letting other people help. Also, contributions from other people can improve the quality of the work with new ideas and concepts.

One good example of this is in doing repairs for your house. If you are the only person doing it, your project takes longer to finish as you have to perform one repair at a time. By hiring a contractor, you allow someone who has experience and skills to do the task for you. Perhaps a team will focus on the living room while another focuses on the roof. As such, you get to cross off multiple items on your to-do list at any given instance. Your only challenge by that time will be funding the entire project. By bringing in new ideas and insights, a productive person finishes tasks on time without sacrificing quality. On the other hand, a busy person will painstakingly go through every step of the lengthy process by him or herself.

5. Busy People Talk About Plans. Productive People Act.

When you ask a busy person what they will do for that day, more often than not, they will respond by giving you a litany of tasks that need to be done by the end of the day. On the other hand, productive people are already making the first step towards clearing that list. A productive person cares little for the approval of everybody and does things at their own pace. After all, people will know that you have done something the moment it is completed. The only time you hear a productive person talk about their tasks is when they have finished them.

6. Busy People Juggle. Productive People Set Boundaries.

A busy person devotes a significant portion of their time and energy to different pursuits all at once. This is quite common if you are younger as you'd want to do a lot of things before you hit your 40s.

However, the more productive approach is to be mindful of what you can actually do and what you can focus on. Establishing a healthy work-life balance is all about setting up boundaries between the different aspects of your life. A productive person understands that he can only do so much without sacrificing time in one part of life. For example, any notion of working overtime only occurs to them when necessary. Alternatively, they also know that their private time is sacred and, if possible, do not take unfinished jobs back home. Anything that was left incomplete will be done in the office the next day. By learning when to stop, a productive person prevents problems from one aspect of their lives from spilling into another.

Effectiveness vs. Efficiency: What's the Difference?

Like being busy and being productive, people also mistake the concept of being effective with being efficient. Both "Effs" are beneficial towards productivity but in different ways. To understand the difference, we should break the words down to their most basic definition. Effectiveness is producing the result as was decided and desired in the most decisive manner possible. However, efficiency is the ability to produce the desired results with minimal waste.

How does this difference relate to the concept of productivity? For that, we need an example. Let us say that there are two SEO companies, A and B. Both companies were successful in ranking the pages of their respective client. In all parameters, they can be deemed "effective" with their strategy employed.

But what about their "efficiency"? Let us say that Company A used a method that took two months to complete and five people with a total price tag of $300.00. But what if Company B used a technique that took only one month to complete and three people for a price of $200.00? By comparison, Company A's method is the less "efficient" alternative. Do not get the wrong idea, though. Both Effs are legitimate methods for getting things done. However, being merely effective is a more restrictive way. If you can do a task involving fewer steps and in a shorter period, what's stopping you from taking that course of action?

The best method here is to set up a baseline of effectiveness first. You can do this by setting up the goals and then the tasks, processes, and resources needed to get that goal accomplished. Once the baseline is set, you can then start optimizing your system. Find out what steps are redundant or need further streamlining. You could even let others help you improve on your system. In short, you should at least be effective in your job. However, you must strive to become more efficient at it.

"Multitasking" And How It Hurts Your Productivity

We have already established that true multitasking does not work for everyone. Your brain can only focus on one task at any given instance. As such, we would focus now on the more popular version of "multitasking", that marathon of different tasks we unconsciously submit ourselves to regularly.

There are two ways that a person "multitasks". The first is the constant shifting from one task to another within any given time. For example, you might be completing an essay in one minute, doing your laundry in another, and taking care of your children next. The other form is giving yourself several tasks in rapid succession. You might be reading an email in one minute, then filing a report, make a cold call to a prospective client in the next, and meeting your department head afterward, with no breaks in between.

What makes either version of multitasking detrimental is that neither of them offers a large margin of success. Only a tiny fraction of multitaskers are genuinely effective in what they do. The rest fail in juggling tasks.

But how does this affect your ability to get things done in general? Here are three ways:

1. It Increases Your Susceptibility towards Distractions.

Remember that multitasking requires a constant shift in goals and roles. This frequent leapfrogging between two tasks will leave you more vulnerable to any distraction that might come your way. You might instinctively act on distractions because you have conditioned your brain to shift between focuses and concerns continually. This increased distractibility is more pronounced in open office spaces, with colleagues talking and moving around. You might be completing a document while a few colleagues are engaged in a heated discussion nearby. With every distraction, your train of thought is stopped. And before carrying on, you have to first deal with the distraction.

2. It Creates a Mental "Bottleneck".

Multitasking might make you more active and productive in the short run, but the mental strain it inflicts on you makes it unsustainable in the long run. Hence, the benefits tend to decline over time. When the backlog of unfinished tasks starts to grow, you will develop a mental bottleneck that saps a lot of your cognitive energy. That mental bottleneck will remain unless you find a way to "unclog" the blockage. Suppose you could not finish a report because you were busy answering emails as soon as they arrived in your inbox. That unfinished report will sit at the back of your brain and continue to bother you until being completed. And while you are getting pestered by the thought, you continue to do other tasks. The end result is that you become unfocused, which leads to more tasks left unfinished or done haphazardly.

3. It Increases Stress Levels.

Usually, the brain increases its output of stress hormones as a natural response to pressure. In this way, it helps the body deal with the stress inflicted on it. However, the body usually has to deal with the side effects once the pressure is gone. At its worst, you may develop a dependency on the stress hormones. This is where that "rush" that some procrastinators are looking for originates.

Multitasking often leaves you vulnerable to this phenomenon as it exposes your body to multiple sources of stress. In essence, it leaves you in bouts of reduced willpower and strength. The constant shifting of goals common to multitasking puts a considerable strain on your mental fortitude and negatively affects your ability to quickly deliver the desired results. Hence, doing away with multitasking is in your best interests in the long-term.

To summarize:

You can be busy and not productive. There is more to being productive than just running around frantically, shifting between tasks, and trying to do many things simultaneously. In this chapter, we discussed why being busy can hurt our productivity and reviewed the differences between being busy and being productive.

Do not get the wrong idea, though. Being busy is something that cannot be avoided in this day and age. Everyone has to deal with their crunch times where they have to deal with more tasks at once. But that is precisely the problem. Those moments of extreme activity should be an exception in your daily life, not the norm.

Think of it this way: remember those fight scenes in the old Bruce Lee movies? It is not the fact that he challenges multiple opponents to an impressive fight. Anybody could do that (and get hammered in 5 seconds). What is remarkable, instead, is that he manages to take them all down eventually. And he does so by being smart on who he takes on every second and how.

You might not find yourself in a bar fight any time in the future, but the same principle applies to productivity. It's not about taking on a lot of tasks at once. Busyness has never been a prerequisite for success. What matters is setting realistic and clear goals, prioritize them, and try to complete as much as possible on time and with minimal waste generated. If you choose to do many things at once, you end up not doing anything at all.

CHAPTER V

THE PITFALLS OF PERFECTIONISM

"Have no fear of perfection – you'll never reach it."

Salvador Dali

Let us say that you have an ongoing project. It may be something like following a course or putting up a new extension to your house. It might be a side job or a new business. Whatever the case, the task you are working on should have been completed by now. This does beg the question: why isn't the task done yet?

Perhaps you keep redoing your plans, starting from scratch with the slightest setbacks. Maybe you did not like the trial output and thus had to go back to the drawing board. Perhaps you have dropped everything because you think that the entire pursuit is a failure despite just being barely halfway-through. That is provided, of course, if you even started on your plans in the first place. Perhaps you are waiting for the "perfect" moment to start on your plans to ensure 100% success. Whatever the case, you have become a slave to the idea of Perfection. Perfectionism can be a rather self-defeating behavior in many ways. Combine this with a tendency towards procrastination, and you have one of the most potent productivity killers to date.

What is Perfectionism?

Perfectionism, in its broadest term, can come in various flavors. It can be a longing for excellence in every aspect of life, a tendency towards controlling and nitpicking, holding yourself to a near-impossible standard, preferring over-delivering on any request, and basing your self-worth on how well you can meet these standards. All of these flavors can limit your productivity by making it challenging to prioritize your time and energy.

Perfectionists often suffer from anxiety. They are worried about many things, such as the following: the outcome not being up to their standards, others judging them unfavorably, underdelivering, and so on. Everything should be under control for perfectionists, and you either succeed or fail - nothing in between. Here's a classic example. You studied for an upcoming exam to get an A+. You did pass, but your grade was an A. Your goal was noteworthy, but your condition for victory was not. For the perfectionist, everything has to be done on their fixed conviction. It is not enough to succeed on a task; you have to do it exceptionally well.

Before we move on, please keep in mind that we are not advocating mediocrity here. Aiming for the best possible results is not an unhealthy attitude. If a person can consistently give high-quality output, then there is no reason to perform less well in any given situation. However, it is not realistic for most of us to regularly deliver impeccable results on everything. Eventually, we often have to prioritize, try to deliver good results on the highest priorities, and be less demanding on low-priority items.

The problem with perfectionism when it comes to productivity is not just the output. It is also the frame of mind it puts a person in. Perfectionism tends to make someone's value contingent on how they achieve their task. In the example above, if your sense of self-worth depends on whether or not you get an A+ for a subject, you will feel like a failure if you get a grade lower than that. In turn, you will have doubts about whether or not you will succeed in the next exams. As a result, you focus on less-threatening activities until you are in the "perfect" mindset again. This is something called Perfection-caused Procrastination.

Regarding procrastination, perfectionism can manifest in several ways like:

- Holding yourself to a high standard
- Having no guarantee that you will do well enough on any task
- Feeling that anything less than the best outcome is not an option
- Discomfort when you feel that you are not doing well enough
- Fearing such feelings of discomfort
- Alleviating such discomfort by engaging in safer activities like browsing social media or playing videogames.
- Repeating the entire process from above until you feel better

Why Perfection Works Against Productivity

As was stated, productivity is about getting things done instead of doing more things. Perfectionism can work against that notion in several different aspects. Here are six examples:

1. Micromanaging

In the workplace, you will encounter many situations where you have to decide or, at least, delegate the decision-making to somebody else. However, a perfectionist cannot even designate whether or not a decision is unimportant. For the perfectionist, any flaw is a project-ending crisis. To any other person, a setback or problem encountered along the process can be shrugged off, worked through, or even incorporated into the overall design. For perfectionists, any problem gives an irritating sensation that won't go away until it is fixed. As such, they'd rather not take the risk and micromanage everything. Every aspect of a task is something worthy of their full attention and effort. They can't leave such important detail to someone else, or everything might go wrong.

2. Over-promising and Over-delivering

The challenge of perfectionism is not to meet everybody's expectations but to meet the self-imposed expectations. The problem with that is what you expect could be way beyond what is reasonable. Let us say that you took on a task and promised to deliver it within 24 hours. However, you suddenly get the idea that you could do better and aim to finish the job in six hours. You could be tempted to deliver more than expected within the agreed time frame. You might think aiming at over-delivering or delivering faster than expected creates a safety margin. In other words, if you aim at twice the required output, you will be able to deliver at least what is expected. A feeling of insecurity could cause this line of thinking. For instance, you think that to prevent others from being disappointed with you, you should always go beyond expectations.

Striving for excellence on its own is a worthy cause. However, it is not a practical approach in everyday life and business due to limitations in time, resources, and mental energy. It is not sustainable to over-promise and over-deliver on every task we take on. Eventually, we all have to designate which tasks are more important and aim at delivering the expected result for those tasks on time. Other tasks could be delegated or completed imperfectly.

3. Being terrified of new situations

Many perfectionists are afraid of "making a fool of themselves" by avoiding new and challenging situations.

This has a lot to do with the way perfectionists approach new challenges. They might first hesitate to try something new because they want to be 100% sure about the outcome. But once that hesitation is gone, they might take everything at once and find out that they have bitten off more than they could chew.

The ability to be flexible and adapt to the new environment is a sign of a sound mind. If your schedule is too regimented, too precise, and too predictable, you are conditioning your mind to provide conventional answers to unconventional situations. The perfectionists turn rigid self-discipline into a compulsion. They inadvertently handicap themselves when a situation calls for an out-of-the-box solution.

4. Chasing excellence excessively

Going back to the drawing board is a natural part of the creative process. However, the perfectionists' problem is that they like to frequent the original plan repeatedly. The end result is that most of their brilliant ideas remain just that: brilliant ideas.

Look no further than in history with the likes of Leonardo da Vinci. Hailed as one of the most brilliant artists and inventors of the Renaissance, a true polymath with vast knowledge about many different fields, including human anatomy, aerodynamics, astrology, theology, painting, sculpture, and many more. But Da

Vinci was quite infamous for taking too long to bring his ideas into reality. And we are not talking about months here, but years. He took more than 16 years to finish the Mona Lisa and had to be threatened with defunding just to finish The Last Supper. Da Vinci had more sketches for brilliant inventions than actual working machines at the end of his life. Most of us do not have Da Vinci's genius. For us, what matters is getting things done with acceptable quality. It is good to strive for excellence in a few critical aspects of every task. But to develop a habit of pursuing excellence for every little detail (regardless of its impact) could become a significant productivity-killer.

5. Unreasonable Standards

What sets Achievers from Perfectionists apart? The answer lies in how high the bar they have set for themselves. An achiever sets a high standard just for the thrill of pushing things a wee bit further once the primary goals have been met. For a perfectionist, the goals are too far to reach from the get-go. For example, you might have set a goal of finishing a project in 6 days while you had a month to complete it. There's a reason for the project length, but you have set this high personal goal that nobody asked you to meet your eagerness to impress.

Setting a very high goal could prevent the perfectionists from enjoying the task. For them, only meeting the goal matters, and the fear of not completing it prevents them from having any semblance of enjoyment from their task. Even worse, if they do not meet their high standards, the perfectionist starts to blame himself.

6. Self-Flagellation over Failure

If failure does occur, a perfectionist takes too much time mulling over what just happened. For them, the inability to complete the goal is mentally crippling, and it takes them quite a while to get back up and be in optimal performing condition. This is quite the opposite of a typical achiever who can quickly bounce back from their mistakes and take failure in a stride. This can be traced back to that victory-contingent self-value that perfectionists place on them concerning the task at hand.

A perfectionist need not even wholly fail at a task to assess themselves negatively. It is enough that somebody did better than them with the same task. As long as that high bar of success is not cleared, their minds would tell they did not fail but, instead, they are a failure. The latter can take quite a while to recover from mentally.

The Stigma of Failure

You might be wondering why we are talking about perfectionists in a book dedicated to unproductive behavior. Aren't they the exact opposite since they strive to be the best at what they do? After all, you can't be a perfectionist if you are not able to produce anything.

The answer lies in the word "Risk". The most basic definition of risk is the probability of one's exposure to any adverse outcome, including harm, loss, or failure. For this chapter, we'd focus on that third outcome: Failure.

When one is accustomed to achieving, the prospect of failing becomes more problematic to them. In essence, when you consistently meet a goal, your tendency towards risk-taking regarding that goal decreases.

This goes back to the perfectionists' tendency to make their self-worth contingent on how they perform or produce output. Since there is only Win or Lose in a perfectionist's frame of mind, they'd rather not put themselves in situations where the latter is likely to occur. Hence, they might decide to avoid the task altogether.

A good example of this is in school. A student who gets used to getting 4.00-grade point averages tends to settle for more "predictable" college courses. This is not because they think they can't handle the challenge, but they would rather not lose that 4.00 streak they have been building since childhood. They also tend to involve themselves less in extra-curricular activities as this might take away time from their studies.

Getting high grades is an admirable goal; there is no doubt about that. However, the fear of failure has prevented the student from taking risks or embracing new challenges. In contrast, students who have wildly varying GPAs (and a few Fs in the past) tend to adopt a "nothing to lose" stance in college and take on riskier subjects.

Now, there is absolutely nothing wrong with risk aversion. Too many risks can expose a person to a lot of predicaments later on. However, the kind of risk we talk about here revolves around new opportunities in life. In essence, risk aversion due to the fear of failure can be detrimental if you cannot take on new opportunities.

Curbing Perfectionism

Fortunately, it is relatively straightforward to deal with the tendency towards perfectionistic procrastination. You can try first to discover the root causes of your perfectionism and address them. To help you out, here are seven tips on dealing with being a perfectionist.

1. Make Getting Started Simpler

Do not wait for perfect conditions to get started because you might end up waiting too long. Due diligence, planning, and preparations are all necessary but to a reasonable level. Many tasks in daily situations will become easier once started. At work, getting the first sketch or the first draft report could help get feedback and refine the idea or the concept.

2. Avoid All-or-Nothing Mentality

Many perfectionists tend to have black and white thinking. If they are anything less than a brilliant success, they are an absolute failure. The real world is not black or white; there are many shades in between. The reality is often complicated and relative. Instead of focusing on getting the best grades, having the most impressive career, or the best relationship, we should focus on being open to learning, gaining new skills, and improving our relationships. The all-or-nothing mentality results in either being overly competitive without any empathy or losing one's self-worth. The opposite of the all-or-nothing mentality is accepting the possibility of achieving results between the two extremes. Learning a new hobby is a good example. You don't need to be a master in that hobby to enjoy it. Just getting good at it is OK!

3. Delegate

Unless you are told so or when everybody else has had their hands full, do not think that you should do your task on your own. You have to realize that, standards notwithstanding, you can only do so much. A few extra hands will help you get motivated to complete a task and go through each phase as quickly as possible. At the same time, extra help gives you the ability to see things from a different perspective. This new perspective can help you understand the task's actual magnitude and long-term costs and benefits. Perhaps, the chances of failing at the task are not as big as you think if you see it from another person's perspective.

4. Break Down Tasks into Smaller Pieces

This is another common pitfall among perfectionists. They tend to look at any task as a single entity, either entirely done or otherwise they have failed. Breaking down a task into smaller sub-tasks makes it easier to get started, gives more frequent feelings of accomplishment, and makes the planning and delegation easier.

5. Stop Comparing

Comparing output has rarely been conducive to productivity. What happens if you look at your co-worker and notice that what they did is different from yours? The chances are that you are going to have doubts about what you have produced and re-do everything. As such, what could have taken half a day to complete has now doubled in completion time.

To avoid comparing output, you should understand the parameters of the task first. Knowing what the project needs from you right from the start will help prevent you from re-doing everything mid-process. Of course, there are tasks whose parameters are so vague that they can be open to interpretation. In this instance, there is nothing that you can do except getting started and pushing through with your project. Usually, the scope and the requirements of such projects become clearer along the way. Comparing is even less helpful for such projects because the end result was not clear from the project start.

6. Keep Your Mind Open to Unconventional Solutions

You always have to remember that, as the saying goes, there are more ways to skin a cat. In projects where you have to collaborate with others, remember that there is more than one "correct" way to solve a problem. In short, what methods work with you might be different from another. As such, give the other person a chance to try out their way while working on yours. At the very least, this prevents you from nitpicking on your or the other person's output. At most, this prevents you from turning into that insufferable know-it-all that saps the energy of everybody involved in the project.

7. Do Not Overdo the Task

If you have agreed to a deadline, you must make sure that you produce the results within that time. This could work two ways. First, you must not rush things through in a misguided attempt to impress your superiors. Take your time to finish each phase and optimize the output before presenting it. Second, once you have finished your task, learn when to STOP working on it. Do not overdo the "finishing touches" just to make things perfect. Instead, review the parameters given to you and determine if your output, at the very least, meets all of them. In all cases, be mindful of the pace that you are doing your work. Do not take too much or too little time.

The Failure Test

Believe it or not, there is a way to tackle the perfectionist line of thinking. The main hurdle is the fear that everything will fall apart if you stop chasing perfection. Perfectionists strongly believe in their stride for excellence and highly value it. To start questioning this belief is a real challenge for them.

To do what was mentioned above, you need to do a little bit of an experiment. Find an activity that you know you can perform well. For this instance, we'd use something competitive like bowling as it pits you with another person. The first question you have to ask yourself is this "Do I like what I am doing?". It's one thing to do your activity well. That's the easy part. Finding out if you are enjoying what you are doing will take a bit of introspection.

Most of the time, you enjoy what you are doing if you are motivated to complete it. Perhaps in bowling, you enjoy the sight of a strike or the actual physical exertion involved as you roll that ball through the lane. Pleasure is something that cannot be forced upon you. It only happens if your brain actually likes whatever task it is doing. This will help you understand that not every task out there has to be done by you. There are some activities that only you can do and others that you can delegate to others. The point is that you know what you can do and in what way you can finish that task without making yourself miserable.

The next step is going to be a bit hard: deliberately miss a shot. Throw at the wrong angle or deliberately aim for the gutter. Once that ball misses, now watch your opponent. What was his reaction? Probably, he was not even looking at you since he was focused on his lane.

How about you? What did you feel when you missed? Did that missed shot profoundly affect you? If you think about it, that missed shot did not turn you into an uncoordinated mess. Plus, you can still take a second shot and do better.

The point here is that every mistake that you make, willingly or otherwise, does not impact your self-worth at all. In any results-oriented environment, everyone is given a bit of leeway to deal with mistakes. You might get chewed depending on how you failed, but you are always given a chance to do things better. Try to look at failure and mistakes not as defining factors to your self-worth but as learning opportunities. In fact, you can learn more from your screw-ups than from a winning streak.

To summarize:

Do not even get the idea that being a perfectionist equates to being unproductive. The truth is that perfectionists are usually highly motivated and goal-oriented people, and they have a track record of getting things done. Nevertheless, they could fall victim to procrastination too, in their own way.

What happens in perfection-derived procrastination is that the person has the right kind of drive but is fueled by the wrong emotions. Fear of failure and a tendency to place unreasonable standards on oneself can be a rather self-defeating concoction of a personality.

As such, the main problem being posed by perfectionism is not that quality output cannot be achieved but that the path to get there is unnecessarily long and full of backtracking. The perfectionist's challenge is to streamline that decision-making process by doing away with unnecessary nitpicking and over-analysis. Learning to meet expectations first than to overdo such will also help in curbing perfectionism.

Lastly, one must have to understand that success is never guaranteed. Even with the best-laid plans, there exist the chance that everything will not work in your favor. As such, a perfectionist must gradually learn to take defeat by stride. Once the bar has been knocked a few reasonable levels down, that perfectionist can start to grow from a procrastinator to an on-time achiever.

CHAPTER VI

THE MAGIC OF GOOD HABITS

> *"Motivation is what gets you started. Habit is what keeps you going."*
>
> *Jim Rohn*

So far, we have been talking about why and how we procrastinate, why so many people are not as productive as they want to be, and how some habits like multi-tasking and perfectionism serve as impediments towards getting things done.

From now on, we will discuss how we could curb such habits, mindsets, and attitudes while embracing a more productive perspective. We will take the learnings and shape them into practical solutions to limit procrastinating tendencies and improve productivity.

Why Good Habits Matter

Why should you replace your bad habits with good ones? Oxford Learner's Dictionary defines "Habit" as "a thing that you do often and almost without thinking, especially something hard to stop doing". So, habits are we tend to do regularly, and we are so accustomed to them that we may even not notice anymore. Becoming more productive requires repeatable and consistent changes in the mindset, behavior, and daily routines. It is like a lifestyle change and not a one-time fix. Hence to become productive and to remain that way, you have to develop certain productivity habits. Before talking about productivity habits, let's review a few points here.

1. Habits are Reflections of Your Personality

As mentioned before, habits are a set of tasks that you do without having to think about them. They are our behavior patterns and daily routines that you don't have to second-guess yourself when performing them. However, actions do not become habits unless the mind consciously incorporates them into its usual mental patterns. They are, in essence, manifestations of who you truly are. If you pride yourself in being career-driven, detail-oriented, and productive, that should be seen in your actions. In fact, a productive person does not have to inform the rest of the world that they are productive. The way they conduct themselves consciously and subconsciously will do that for them.

2. Habits Could Be Changed

As much as habits are subconscious actions, they are also replaceable. If one habit you have is no longer working for you or producing the benefits you are looking for, you can replace them with new ones. But there lies a challenge: habits are born slowly and die hard. The good news is that with consistency and willpower, new habits can become second nature to you. The same goes for productivity. You can increase your productivity by curbing your tendency to reach out for your mobile phone and start going through your social media updates. However, that could be hard if you have become dependent on social media for entertainment or validation. But that does not mean to say that you can't drop bad habits. The point is that we should first find out which habits are detrimental to our productivity and realize that changing them will take time and effort.

3. Habits Are Goal-Oriented.

Good Habits are formed for one main reason; because you really want something. In fact, setting a habit is the first step towards reaching a goal. To become productive, you must develop some habits geared toward becoming productive. Regardless of if you choose to focus on increasing output, curbing procrastination, or making yourself more motivated, good habits are always needed to secure these goals as quickly as possible.

4. They Set the Tone of Your Life.

Habits, whether good or bad, often dictate the overall course of your life. If you set up productive habits, you tend to reach more of your goals. The opposite is also true. If you smoke a pack of cigarettes every day, have an unhealthy diet, do little or no physical exercise, and live a stressful life, do you think it is realistic to remain healthy, happy, and physically strong? Our lives will resemble the sum of our habits. As Wil Durant said in a famous quote, "we are what we repeatedly do. Excellence, then, is not an act, but a habit".

5. Habits are a Great Alternative to Motivation

A habit can help you overcome that obstacle of finding the "right mood" to do anything. This is because that habit is ingrained in your memory and becomes your automatic responses. You will do them without having to go through an internal debate on the pros and cons of such an action. Since you do these on autopilot, you need not have to wait for the right mental condition. In fact, the most productive people do not have to wait to get motivated to do something. They go through their usual daily routine, and tasks get done as a direct consequence. If you adopt a few productive behaviors, do them regularly, and let them develop into habits, you do not need to motivate yourself every time. Once a habit is formed, you can just let it happen.

What Productivity Looks Like

Now that we know how procrastination and productivity manifest in day-to-day living, you might wonder what being productive looks like. As we discussed before, productivity is not the same as being busy, exhausted, or always in action. There is more to productivity than just doing more or trying to make use of every second of the day. Sometimes the most productive use of your time is to take more rest. That is because productivity is more about being effective than being overly prolific.

Let's explain this with an example. Which of the following scenarios do you consider as being more productive?

- **Scenario 1**: Spending double the usual time to prepare a perfect report with all little details worked out, finishing the report late at night, feeling exhausted, no time left to spend with the family, going to sleep after midnight, waking up tired the next day.

- **Scenario 2**: Getting the most important parts of the report right, completing the rest with reasonable quality, finishing it off in the working hours, spending some time with your family, going to bed in time, waking up fresh.

It would be difficult to argue that the first scenario is more productive. Maybe the output is a bit neater. But how much of an impact does that make? Most probably not so much. While the first scenario is a typical example of a perfectionist attitude, the second scenario portrays effectiveness.

Productivity is more about effectively working towards your personal and professional goals. It starts with choosing your goals carefully, whether your long-term and major life goals or your daily to-do list. This is where prioritization becomes essential. After all, being effective is meaningless without choosing the right goals. Our valuable resources, such as time, mental energy, and budget, are all limited. Once the goals are correctly set, we can think of spending our resources effectively and become more productive.

You might think of productive people as robots that can swiftly and effortlessly complete task after task. The truth is that productive people not only set their goals correctly and spend their resources effectively, but they also have certain habits that allow them to get more done efficiently and consistently. Forming good habits has a cascade effect on your productivity. They allow you to be more efficient, which means you can get things done in less time. Hence, you will have more time to learn new things, develop new habits, get more done, etc. The opposite is also true, of course.

Now that we know how important it is to form habits, here are fifteen tips to strengthen your existing good habits and create new ones. The goal here is to make gradual changes to get lasting effects. That needs patience and perseverance. So, please remember to stay realistic and be kind to yourself!

1. The Most Important Task Approach

Prioritization is an essential habit of productivity and could be applied over different time horizons and personal and professional lives. Just checking off tasks as they are written in order will not do much since you will mix essential tasks with non-essential tasks.

The Most Important Tasks (MIT) approach will come in handy as you identify which of the tasks have the most significant impact. This approach could be applied to shorter time frames, such as the daily to-do list or longer terms and broader life goals. The theory behind this is that not all tasks in a day have the same impact. Some must be done ASAP, and others can be done at a later, more convenient time. Without something to delineate the tasks according to importance, you might end up spending your mental energies on non-essential activities for that day.

The MIT Approach also helps expose a common procrastination trait, focusing on non-essential activities instead of important ones. You might be checking tasks off for a specific day, but they might not actually matter so much or contribute a lot to your weekly or monthly goals. The MIT Approach requires you to sit down and spend a few minutes at the start of the day to choose 1 to 3 MITs. Consider what tasks for that day must be done. Will it be an appointment with your doctor or lawyer? Will it be unclogging that kitchen sink? Will it be filing the Income Tax Return? Whatever it is, you must identify them before you start your day.

2. Do Not Mix Importance and Urgency

When setting your priorities, it is essential to distinguish the importance of a task from its urgency because they are not necessarily the same. A task might be important, but it is not urgent. On the other hand, a task might be seemingly urgent but not important.

You can use the Eisenhower Priority Model to determine how much of a priority or importance a particular activity should get. Named after the 34th US President Dwight Eisenhower (who was a highly productive person!), the Eisenhower Priority Model can help you identify which tasks need to be done first. Interpreting this model is rather easy and is as follows:

A. If a task is important and urgent, do it NOW.

B. If a task is important but not urgent, schedule a time to do it LATER.

C. If a task is not important but urgent, DELEGATE it to somebody else.

D. If a task is not important and not urgent, ELIMINATE it.

Tasks in Group A usually have precise deadlines, and not acting on them could have consequences. Finishing a client project or picking up your kid from the schools fall in this group.

Tasks in Group B are important to reaching your goals (in the short or long term) but do not have a set deadline, making them easy to procrastinate on. Getting physical exercise, planning for your professional development, or developing new products to remain competitive are examples from this group. Items in this group usually require thoughtful and long-term planning. They bring value to our personal and professional lives and vary from person to person.

Tasks in Group C have to be done within a reasonable time but not necessarily by you. For example, you need to eat every day, but the meal does not need to be cooked by you.

Most tasks in Group D are distractions and should be limited or eliminated. Think about watching TV or playing video games. This group of tasks provides excellent procrastinating opportunities.

Let's assume that you are in an office and have only one hour to do the following:

- Finish a client report which is due tomorrow
- Prepare a presentation for the next team meeting
- Prepare and email photocopies of old documents to a colleague

At the same time, you have several distractions, such as the following:

- Idle chatter with office mates
- Checking social media updates
- Read non-essential emails

Using the Eisenhower Model, you can place Task "Finish the report" in Group A (Do it now!) and

"Prepare the presentation" in Group B (find time to do it later). For the "prepare photocopies" task, you should put that in Group C. Perhaps one of the office interns can assist you with the photocopies while performing the first two activities. As for the distractions, you would have to put them in Group D; in other words, avoid or eliminate them.

The Eisenhower Model is great for categorizing your tasks and helping you understand which groups you tend to focus your energies on. If you tend to spend more time on tasks that are not on the first two groups, it is high time for you to reconsider your priorities.

But what if you are faced with many different choices with varying degrees of urgency and importance? How can you apply the Eisenhower Model in complicated real-life situations? The main challenge in using the Eisenhower Model is the so-called "Mere-Urgency Effect", as discussed by Meng Zhu and her colleagues in Johns Hopkins Business School in a 2018 article in Journal of Consumer Research. The Mere-Urgency Effect is our tendency to prioritize tasks with a deadline, even if they are not so important. The deadline here could even be a feeling spurious urgency. For example, we know that social media updates have some sort of expiry date. In other words, they will be outdated or proved wrong if we check them a few days or even a few hours later. This illusionary sense of urgency can distort our process of setting priorities. The good news is that the same study showed our tendency to prioritize urgency over importance could be controlled if we think enough about the consequences and our choices' pay-off. Next time, the Mere-Urgency Effect tempted you to procrastinate on the important but non-urgent tasks and think about what really matters!

3. Deep Work

There are some tasks which could be done while you are busy doing something else simultaneously. For example, you can drive while listening to music or water the plants while talking to your neighbor. This is not the same as multitasking. It is just that the task does not require your total attention and could be done together with something else. On the other hand, some tasks need focus. They may be complicated or intricate or might have a strict time limit. You cannot complete these tasks haphazardly. You will need serious time and effort to get them done. This is called "deep work" and it is a hallmark of productive people. In essence, you have to put yourself in a state of mind where your focus is on nothing else but the task in front of you. Here are four tips to perform deep work:

A. Schedule Smartly

Since deep work consumes tremendous amounts of mental energy, you must put them in a time of the day where your brain is functioning at its peak. This might be morning for some people or later in the afternoon for others. To make a habit of deep work, you better be consistent with your scheduling. If you decide to perform deep work in a specific part of the day, make sure you do it as much as possible at approximately the same time. This conditions your mind to work at its peak level at that time every day.

B. Use Boredom to Your Advantage

This might sound counterproductive, but boredom can be used as a motivator to do deep work. How this works is tricky but easy to pull off. Essentially, deep work is not meant to be enjoyable, which is why our brains will look for distractions. When your brain is looking for distractions, its focus is taken off from doing the task at hand. As such, you must get yourself "bored" enough to do that task by taking away all your distractions. No social media, no phone, no games. Nothing. With nothing else to take your mind away from the task at hand, the chances of finishing that task will increases.

C. Be Harder to Get Contacted

Although becoming anti-social is never recommended in the workplace, you can still find ways to respectfully tell other people not to bother you when focusing on deep work. For instance, you can ask colleagues to email you instead of calling you or trying to talk to you in person. You can also inform your colleagues, teammates, and manager that you need to focus during that day or part of the day and politely ask them to help you not be disturbed. Another solution could be to work in a more isolated part of the workplace (or work from home). The same principle applies to being contacted by email, phone, video calls, etc. It would be best if you can totally isolate and disconnect yourself for the deep work duration.

D. Understand How You Work

In what condition do you find yourself performing at optimum levels? Perhaps you are the type of worker that gets things done in complete silence. Maybe you are the worker that needs periodic breaks. Whatever the case, you should understand your working preferences and try to find ways to create conditions in which you can work optimally. You do not need to do away with your schedules to do deep work. You just have to set aside the available time you have to focus on these tasks.

4. Know What Distracts You

Distractions are some of the biggest hurdles you will have to clear when it comes to productivity. The fact that they surround us these days and come in different forms does not help either. Nevertheless, you can still work your way around them. The first step to combat distractions is to recognize what they are. They can range from social media to emails and from co-workers dropping by to smoking and coffee breaks. Sometimes too many meetings could become a significant distraction. Working from home can create its own distractions, from kids running around or continually asking for attention to your pet making a mess.

Once recognized, you do not need to act immediately. Instead, you can take note of the distraction. This helps to let you identify what bothered you at that moment without taking you away from your current task. For example, you might be in the middle of work when you suddenly remembered having to pay the bills. Paying your bills requires attention, but it doesn't deserve it right now. Perhaps you can deal with that later in your free time.

You might not be able to change the world around you entirely according to your preferences, especially if you have co-workers or work in a big open office. Nevertheless, you can still make some adjustments in your working schedule, choose another desk or office for a few hours, put your mobile phone aside, answer non-essential emails later, and so on. With a little bit of creativity, you can certainly bring at least some of the distractors under control.

5. Have A Plan for Your Day (or a week, month, etc.)

One of the most useful productivity habits is to plan what you want to do in a specific time frame. Creating such a habit will encourage you to think about the urgency and the importance of any task you will take on. Furthermore, having a plan prepares your mind to engage better and faster with the tasks. It also makes it easier to say "No" to demands for which you have no time. The goal here is to start the day with an idea of what you want to achieve on that day. This idea could become more concrete by writing down a to-do list.

6. Include Buffer Time in Your Plan

We just talked about having a plan (for example, a daily to-do list) to improve our productivity. However, such a plan should not attempt to fill every minute of the day. Life is unpredictable; we don't know what might come up that day. Maybe a couple of meetings overrun, or the report you are finishing takes more time.

Considering some buffer time in your plans will allow for the unexpected. It will prevent you from being exhausted and stress out and will eventually improve your productivity. If everything goes according to the plans, you will focus on long-term improvements, get a head start on the next tasks, or take a break and relax!

7. Get Started

Procrastinators have to "get in the mood" before they could start working. You can use this to your advantage by flipping the entire script. Instead of focusing on getting motivated, you should focus on getting started, motivated, or not.

In this part, it is best to use a trick that productive writers use: Let the start mold the story. That means you don't have to worry about the entire scope of the project. Just focus on finishing the first part, and the rest of the concept should follow.

Look at JK Rowling as an example. Back in 1990, she never had an idea for a seven-book series. She didn't even have an idea for one book. All that she had was her inspiration for a magical train ride from King's Cross to Manchester. It was barely a premise for something. But, somehow, she managed to build a story around that train ride which, after many edits and rejections, became Harry Potter and the Philosopher's Stone in 1997, and that book gave birth to a franchise. The point is to not focus too much on the entire process but on getting started. What you have to understand is that action tends to be self-sustaining. Acting is what leads to motivation, which, in turn, inspires more action.

8. Start Small and Continue Step By Step

One of the most significant factors towards procrastination is the very nature of the task itself. Perhaps it is too daunting, too technical, too complicated, or too lengthy. Either way, you find the task just a bit too much for you to handle.

A neat trick you can use is to break the task down into smaller pieces to make it easier to get started. Say, for example, that you are required to write a 5000-word essay. How about starting with an internet search on the topic and trying to find some interesting articles? Think of it as regular web browsing; no outlining, no writing, no editing, nothing overwhelming. Soon you will come across interesting sources, get ideas for the essay outline, choose the most relevant resources, and so on. At this stage, the task will look much more manageable than when you started. The rest of the task could be completed in the same way; in other words, by incremental steps all towards getting the bigger task done.

9. Make Fewer Trivial Decisions

What exactly is a trivial decision? It is those decisions you make that have little impact on your day. Remember that you have only a finite source of mental energy every day, and you should save that up for important and urgent decisions. A good example of a trivial decision is what to wear for work. Is that shirt in season? Does it make you look fat? Any of these questions will make you waste minutes. Many highly productive people have eliminated this triviality by just choosing to wear the same clothing type every day. For example, Steve Jobs used to wear the same black turtleneck, jeans, and white shoes every time he appeared in public. The point of this habit is to conserve your decision-making energies for situations that require them.

10. Delegate

Which of your tasks could be done simultaneously? Here, we don't mean multitasking. Instead, we are talking about letting others do the task for you. For example, look at the kitchens of Michelin Star chefs like Gordon Ramsay and Alain Ducasse. Every person in that kitchen is doing something. One section might be doing the meat, another does the starters, another for food prep, and another for plating and quality check. You don't have to do everything by yourself. Let others focus on one part so you could do the others, saving you time and energy. A production line is a far more efficient system than a one-man show. Delegation is like leveraging the power of a team.

11. Saying No the Right Way

It's easy to get excited about new opportunities and projects. After all, those are chances for you to learn new things or, if you're career-oriented, move one level higher in the organizational ladder. But being a Yes man can carry the risk of you dealing with too many commitments.

This goes back to prioritization. We all have limited time and energy and have to use them carefully. Once we have determined our high priority tasks and plan to do them, you have to decline some other requests diplomatically. The keyword here is "diplomatically" because you can't just tell anyone asking for your help, "No!". Knowing the politest way to say no is one way to alleviate pressure from your work without leaving the entire door closed for future interactions. After all, how would you feel if you need help in the future and nobody would take you on your request for delegation?

Sometimes, you also have to say No to yourself. There are instances when you will be compelled to do one activity or another. Perhaps you would rather be doing low-value, comfortable tasks instead of a more pressing, high-stakes task with long-term benefits. Saying no to the former so you could do the latter should help you get that task off your to-do list successfully and meet your overall goals.

12. Ignore Impulses

The most problematic habit you might have to replace will be the tendency to drop your work and quickly respond to any distraction. For instance, you might be in the middle of writing a report but get the notification of a new email. Probably, there will be that part of your brain telling you, "Hey, open it. Maybe it's something important!". Admittedly, this is a simple matter of prioritizing and maintaining focus. Perhaps that notification is important, or maybe it is not. Usually, you immediately know that. Unless your manager asks an urgent question or there is a personal emergency, you better wait until the task at hand is sufficiently completed. Otherwise, you might end up jumping back and forth between various tasks so much that you will sabotage your productivity.

13. Replenish Your Energy

Remember that you have a finite amount of willpower, energy, and time every day. In other words, you can only do so much effectively at any given time. This is why you have to be careful where you will devote your energies the most to make your day productive.

It might sound counterproductive to everything you have learned so far, but you have to take frequent breaks so that your mind and body can replenish their strength. For starters, you need to get enough sleep every day, say around eight hours. You should also use scheduled break times to your advantage. A common mistake many workers make is to use that break time to do extra work.

That would be a rather admirable effort, but you have to give your brain and body chances to rest in between periods of action.

No matter how good you are, the sheer monotony of doing the same thing over and over again is going to be detrimental to your mind. You can break this cycle by actually making unwinding a legitimate part of your to-do list. This could be a workout in the gym, watching a movie, meeting friends, going on holiday, and so on. You can make yourself feel less guilty about taking a break by making them an actual objective you have to accomplish. At most, this helps in allowing your body to replenish its energies. At the very least, it can help in preventing you from developing some negative emotions regarding the tasks that you usually have to perform.

14. Use Journaling and Its Benefits

Having to write down your thoughts could seem to be far off on learning how to be productive. But, surprisingly enough, it could be a tool to help you improve your mental strength. In a sense, it can help you become productive, depending on how you view the entire concept of journaling.

Journaling can help you become more productive in various ways. Studies have shown that writing your thoughts is an excellent way to cope with stress and anxiety. But why is this so? The answer lies in what happens in our brains when we write. Our short-term memory is somewhat limited. At best, the brain can only hold on to 5 to 7 strands of short-term memories at a time. Anything more will overwhelm most of us. By writing things down, you clear out a bit of that storage and could think more clearly. Without having to hold short-term thoughts since they are written somewhere else regularly, your brain does not have to go over the same thought cycles again and again.

Writing things down in a journal helps your mind cope with these experiences by allowing it to frame things from a different perspective, helping the brain find ways to learn from the experience. Once that awful experience turns into a learning experience, it will not linger in your brain and become a source for your procrastination.

It does sound forced and cliched to claim that writing your goals gives you a better chance of achieving them. However, it does prove to be successful, but not in some weird, mantra-ish way. A plan like "finish report by 5 pm" will remain an idea in your brain for a particular day. You can choose to do whatever with it, even forgetting about it. But by writing things down, you allow the more logical part of your brain to work by asking questions like:

- What do I exactly want?
- How do I go about achieving what I want?
- How long should I perform this task?
- What are my conditions for success or failure?

- How important is this goal compared to others?

And so on.

By writing things down, you allow yourself to be a bit more self-reflective with your actions. A journal helps you understand what you should do and prioritize on any given day. Since your plans are now in writing, you have a tangible channel to track your progress. Are you still achieving your goals? Are you in the right direction? Your journal will tell you exactly that.

Going back to that example of having a bad day, journaling helps you cope with your emotions by giving you a place to vent out your feelings. Do keep in mind that negative feelings regarding specific experiences or tasks occur because such emotions have never been addressed. For instance, you hate doing a task because you hate the person usually giving it. By writing down your feelings regarding these tasks, you allow such emotions to run their course and out of your system. Sure, you might not like the person or the task any better, but at least you got to deal with your emotions in a non-destructive manner. By writing your negative experiences down, you allow yourself to deal with your negative emotions and move on faster. In theory, this should help you recover emotionally without resorting to procrastination.

15. Reflect and Introspect

Spending a few minutes every day on thoughtful reflection could help us learn from our mistakes and get a sense of fulfillment from our achievements. We can look back and think about how well we acted on that day and in which ways we can improve ourselves. This reflection process could be combined with the journaling habit to make sure the learnings will be preserved. Creating such a habit could help us become a better version of ourselves gradually, become mentally and emotionally more stable, and develop a learning mindset.

To summarize:

Good habits can significantly improve your productivity. However, habits do not become habits without one indispensable element: consistent application. At the very least, good habits are strategies, choices that you have to consciously make and apply to generate the results that you were expecting. But they do not become part of your lifestyle unless you consistently apply them. You can't become productive just by choosing to use these strategies for one time and one time only. Instead, you would have to decide to incorporate them into your daily routine consciously. You would know that such productivity habits have become part of your life if you consistently perform them without your mind having to debate itself on their merits.

Chapter VII

Productivity Boost Using the 80/20 Principle

> *If we did realize the difference between the vital few and the trivial many in all aspects of our lives, and if we did something about it, we could multiply anything that we valued.*
>
> Richard Koch

As you find ways to become productive, you might come across a problem. Regardless of how you formulate it, the core of the problem will always remain the same. It goes something like: "How Much Effort Should I Make to Accomplish my Tasks?"

Remember that you can only do so much in a day. How much you can achieve in a day will depend on how well you utilize your limited time and energy resources. But that is precisely the problem. How do you go about making sure that all your efforts do lead to the accomplishment of something? Conversely, how would you know that you are wasting your efforts on something that yields minimal results? If you do not pay enough attention to such questions, you might achieve very little despite your hard work.

Hard work is almost always needed. But it does not guarantee satisfactory outcomes. What matters is what you work on. You want to focus on tasks that give you the highest return and have the most significant impact on achieving your goals. We already talked about prioritization as an essential productivity habit and discussed the Eisenhower Model. When prioritizing your tasks using the Eisenhower Model, it is vital to keep in mind that the impact and the outcome of various tasks are usually not evenly distributed.

This imbalance is present in all aspects of our lives. Have you noticed that you do not use all clothes in your wardrobe equally? Or that a few attendants make most of the comments in a typical meeting, while others are relatively quiet? This observation that most of the outputs are generated by a minority of the inputs was first made by the Italian economist Vilfredo Pareto. Over time, others added to this observation and called it the Pareto Principle. This book discusses the Parteo Principle by its more popular name: the 80/20 principle or the 80/20 rule.

What is the 80/20 Principle?

In 1896, Vilfredo Parteo published his work *Cours d'économie politique*, in which he included his observation on wealth distribution. He noticed that 80% of Italy's wealth was owned by 20% of the population. He tried to prove that this was not specific to Italy and that there was a consistent pattern of wealth distribution in all parts of the world throughout history. In 1906, Parteo had another observation. He saw that roughly 20% of the peapods in his garden contained around 80% of peas. He called this Parteo Distribution and linked it to his previously-published work on wealth distribution.

In 1937, Dr. Joseph Juran (a quality control guru) stated that Pareto's observation regarding wealth distribution also applies to product defects, meaning that 20% of defects cause 80% of the rejected products. Juran called his observation the Pareto Principle and concluded that the quality control systems should focus on removing that 20% of the defects. In this way, a significant improvement in product quality will be achieved with minimal effort. Joseph Juran was the first to point out that his observations and those made by Parteo are not random. Instead, they are like a universal principle. Simply put, this principle states that when many factors, inputs, or factors contribute to a particular output, a limited number of those factors account for the most significant impacts on the output. Dr. Juran also coined the terms "vital few" to refer to those few key contributors and "useful many" or "trivial many" to the rest of the low-impact input factors.

The Pareto Principle has been observed in many areas with roughly the same 80/20 distribution of outcomes. In other words, the same imbalance of outcomes has shown up consistently in various environments. Here are some examples:

- 20% of what students study comprise 80% of what they encounter in a test.

- 20% of the calls made by a sales representative would comprise 80% of their successful sales.

- 20% of interactions with customers would comprise 80% of the total profit.

- 20% of the entire population of patients in a hospital would account for 80% of that facility's healthcare costs.

We see similar uneven distributions in our daily lives. Perhaps the following examples sound familiar to you:

- If your wardrobe has 40 shirts, you might be wearing the same ten shirts every week.
- Of the 20 programs you have installed on your computer, you might only use 4 of them regularly.
- Of the 30 spices and condiments in your pantry, you will only use 6 of them regularly for your meals.
- If your circle of friends contains 50 people, the chances are that you regularly interact with only 10 of them.
- If your house has five rooms, the chances are that you spend most of your day time in one of them.
- The 20% most frequently-used words account for 80% of the word occurrences.

What does this all mean, then? It merely tells you that 20% of what you do, own, and use yields the most impact in your life. These are the "vital few". The rest are either the "useful many" or most probably the "trivial many". A rather straightforward interpretation of the 80/20 principle is that a few things are essential in most cases, and the rest are not. Accepting the 80/20 principle could have significant implications for our productivity and even for how we live our lives in general. This chapter will discuss how we can benefit from the 80/20 principle to boost your productivity by focusing on the "vital few".

Boosting Your Productivity Using the 80/20 Principle

Suppose we accept that the 80/20 rule is a universal principle. In that case, it should be possible to improve our productivity in personal and professional life by focusing on getting the vital 20% of the tasks done. To have a more detailed discussion on how exactly one can use the 80/20 principle to boost productivity, let's first think about what productivity is. The Oxford Dictionary defines productivity as follows: "The rate at which a worker, a company, or a country produces goods, and the amount produced, compared with how much time, work, and money is needed to produce them."

Productivity is about the ratio between the amount of time, work, and money consumed (i.e., the inputs) and the particular result or output. In other words, becoming more productive means either generating more output with a fixed amount of inputs or achieving the desired output with the least amount of inputs. The 80/20 principle has precisely the same goals. For example, if 80% of your company's sales come from 20% of the clients, you can focus your advertising campaigns or your customer service resources on that vital 20 % of customers to increase the sales. In this way, higher outputs could be achieved by using the same inputs. Similarly, suppose your company likes to reduce the costs without sacrificing the revenue. In that case, you can focus on the vital 20% of the products or customers and cut the costs across the other 80%. In this way, less input gets almost the same output. A similar line of thinking could be applied to losing weight, deciding who to spend your free time with, your to-do list at work, and so on.

The above definition and discussions make it clearer why being busy is not the same as being productive. Applying the 80/20 principle to your work and life makes you less busy because you cut on the 80% low-productivity tasks. With more free time, you can focus more on long-term goals, learn new skills, have a healthier lifestyle, and improve your work-life balance. All of these will improve your quality of life, enhancing your focus and boosting your productivity further.

Implementing the 80/20 Principle

Before talking about implementing the 80/20 principle, you need to keep a few notes in mind. The first one is the 80/20 rule is an empirical observation and not something like a law of physics. A large body of experimental evidence supports it, which makes it quite reliable. Nevertheless, attempts to apply this principle to all aspects of life, such as politics or sociology, has received some criticisms. The second note is that the values of 80 and 20 percent are indications rather than fixed numbers. The core premise of Pareto Principle is the imbalance between the inputs and the outputs in many systems; that a minority of inputs or factors account for a disproportionately large percentage of the results. Depending on the topic, the ratio could be 80 and 20, 90 and 10, 70 and 30, or anything in between. The exact numbers do not make a difference. The takeaway message from the 80/20 principle is that the relationship between the inputs and the outputs is usually non-linear. This message can drastically change the way we look at life in general. We tend to think that 50% of our efforts result in 50% of what we achieve. However, the empirical observations formulated in the 80/20 principle reject this 50-50 mindset. The third point is if you want to implement the 80/20 principle as an easy to use guide for your daily life, you should always ask yourself this question: "Which 20% of my daily, weekly or regular tasks bring you more value, success, or happiness?" To measure the value or success, you can use any appropriate metric, for example, how much sales or profit you make or how much free time you have. Furthermore, you can choose your 20% vital tasks by analysis and investigation or intuition and observation.

Carrying out such a universal principle will call upon everything we have talked about so far, from overcoming procrastination and getting started to setting the right priorities and adopting good habits. In the following section, we will discuss four guidelines for successfully implementing the 80/20 principle in your personal and professional lives. The focus of our discussion here is using the 80/20 principle to improve productivity.

1. Identify Your 80/20 Path

Assuming that you already have identified your priorities, i.e., your vital 20%, you should now identify the path towards them. Regardless of your chosen strategy, there are only four possible paths that you could take, which are:

- Low in Effort and Low in Reward
- High in Effort but Low in Reward
- High in Effort and High in Reward
- Low in Effort but High in Reward

If your answer is the 4th route, you are well on the way to mastering the 80/20 rule, i.e., the most straightforward route you could take to get maximum results with comparatively low effort. To help you better understand this path, let us assume that you are a student who needs to pass a major subject for the semester. As such, passing that subject is among your vital 20% of the tasks. You can take the following four possible paths:

1. *Low in Effort and Low in Reward:* Do all of your studying at the last minute.

2. *High in Effort but Low in Reward:* Attend all classes but do not pay attention or set up a timetable for studies but do not exert effort in following it.

3. *High in Effort and High in Reward:* Attend all lectures, pay attention, study for many hours each day, do all the

assignments, review the notes you have taken as well as sample questions and the correct answers.

4. *Low in Effort but High in Reward:* Attend all key lectures and understand each topic's core principle. Go through your past papers to determine which topics will come out in the upcoming exams, and study for retention.

Out of the four possible paths you can take, you are most probably interested in the two high reward paths, and out of those two, route #4 is the most advantageous for you.

The same goes for every project/task/goal that you have to accomplish. Regardless of the strategy, there are only four routes that you can take, and only one of them will yield you the best possible return on investment. Hence, you have to ask yourself what all the possible paths you can take are and, out of those strategies, which one follows the 80/20 rule?

2. Know Your 80/20 Assets

The first step in implementing the 80/20 principle is to know your priorities (i.e., your vital 20%) and choose the right path towards them. Once you have that knowledge, you need some tools to enable you along the way. These tools or assets are in various aspects of your life, such as your mindset, habits, health, and work. It will help if you recognize such assets and leverage them to get you started along the 82/20 path. As you go, you can develop more assets and progress faster. To help you find your 80/20 assets, think about the following points:

- **Your Habits:** We talked about productivity habits in Chapter VI. Which of those habits do you currently have? Are there any habits that you need to do away with?

- **Thoughts:** Try journaling to take note of the usual thoughts that run through your mind. Which ones make you feel good, and which ones tend to demotivate you from work? What are the 20% high-value thoughts that help you keep focus, and which ones are the 80% low-value ones you have to eliminate from your system?

- **Your Health:** The truth is that your overall physical condition can assist or hinder in applying the 80/20 rule. Your health determines how much focus you can maintain and how much effort you can exert. Hence, adopting a healthy lifestyle is essential in applying the 80/20 principle.

- **Your Work:** Whether you want to achieve personal or professional goals, your work experiences, colleagues, on-the-job training, professional network, and so on, could all become your assets along the 80/20 path. Again you should find out what aspects of your work you should focus on to help you reach your goals.

- **Income:** This one is closely related to your work and habits. Which of the tasks you usually perform or the activities you engage in generate most of your income? What can you do to focus more on them to increase your profits there? If you are an employee, what are the key elements of your work that directly affects your monthly salary? And how can you focus on those elements to increase your paycheck?

3. Know your roadblocks

Focusing on the vital 20% is the core premise of the 80/20 principle. You like to follow this principle and get as much as possible done with as little effort as possible. But what if you are blocked along this way? What are you going to do then? For example, you have identified your 20% important tasks, but you must complete many other tasks first. You know that getting enough physical exercise is essential, but you have to take the kids to the playground at the same time. You want to finish a client report. But the loud chatter in the office distracts you.

The point here is that our mere intention to implement the 80/20 rule in our lives is not necessarily enough. You need to identify the roadblocks along the way and try to find solutions for them. Being flexible and creative is essential here. Sometimes we can get help from family and friends. They can help us out with the kids or other personal and professional matters. At work, think about delegating more trivial tasks or building some slack time into your daily or weekly plans. If you work from home, choose a specific area as your home office and reduce the noise and the distractions. Adjusting your daily routines at home and work could remove some of the roadblocks. Maybe you can start working earlier or finish later when the home or the office is quieter.

Choosing your 80/20 path is just the start. You also have to understand which aspects of your life are not compatible with that path and try to adjust them. You have to be realistic, flexible, and creative. Everyone has their battles, with their challenges and opportunities. Always try to keep your vital 20% and the roadblocks in achieving them in mind, in both personal and professional life. If you decide to adopt an 80/20 approach to your life and identify and address possible roadblocks along the path, the chances are high that you will soon see noticeable improvements in your productivity.

4. Think about how to handle the 80%

This chapter's main message so far has been to identify and prioritize your 20% vital tasks and try to recognize and address the roadblocks in your 80/20 path. Maybe you are thinking to yourself: well, that sounds great. But what about the 80% useful or trivial many? That is, in fact, a great question! Identifying and addressing what hinders you from focusing on the vital 20% is essential. But it is equally important to think about how you handle the other 80% of the tasks you face daily.

If you can avoid some of the trivial tasks altogether, you should start there. Think about watching TV or playing videogames for hours, spending a lot of time on social media, too many coffee breaks or random talks at work, and so on. If you have the willpower to eliminate all the trivial or distracting activities from your life, good for you! Otherwise, engaging in any of the activities mentioned above is fine, as long as they are done in moderation.

The next step is to use the Eisenhower Model to delegate or reschedule some other tasks in both personal and professional lives. Which tasks to delegate or reschedule is up to you and your circumstances. Getting help from friends and family, hiring professionals, and leveraging your team's power at work are examples.

The final point to keep in mind about approaching the 80% is to avoid perfectionism. If you want to do everything with perfection, you consider everything vital, and that is simply not compatible with the observations formulated in the 80/20 principle. Some of the tasks on the 80% bucket could be skipped or delegated. Hence, you will not do them at all. For the remainder of the 80% tasks, you should aim to get them done with sufficient quality, not with perfection. Remember that even if all the 80% tasks are done perfectly, they generate roughly

20% of your private or professional life outputs. If you like perfection, get the vital 20% done perfectly! We will talk more about perfectionism and how it can lower your productivity in the next chapter.

How NOT to Apply the 80/20 Rule

It is important to remember that the 80/20 Rule is simply just that, a rule. Hence, it is often open to interpretation, so there are many misapplications of the principle. When you try to apply the 80/20 Rule in your life, you should be mindful of the following points.

1. Getting Caught in the Numbers

With this principle, a rookie mistake is thinking that the 20% or the 80% are fixed values and cannot change. For example, you may refuse to apply the 80/20 rule because you found out that only 10% of your work is vital, not 20%. What matters is the spirit and the concept behind this rule; that a minority of the inputs control the majority of the outputs. The minority could be more than 20% or less than 20% of the inputs. The same goes for the percentage of the outputs. Had Pareto found another distribution ratio, the rule could have been simply called the 10/90 or the 1/2 or the 99/1 rule. The point is that you should not focus too much on reconciling the actual output and input volume you generate. Just understand that there is an inherent mathematical imbalance, and you should use that to your advantage.

2. Recursive Application

This is one of the seemingly thoughtful rebuttals of the application, positing that you would eventually end up with nothing if you keep applying the 80/20 rule. If you find out which of your tasks belong to the vital 20%, you might even look at which part of that 20% belongs to a more vital 20%. Out of the five essential tasks you discovered, you will end up with just one very vital task if you apply the rule again.

This is an interpretation of the rule that relies too much on mathematical analysis. Once you found out which tasks have a more significant impact, stop down-selecting them further. Instead, focus on getting them done so that you can move on to the remaining 80% of the tasks. To prevent making such a mistake, keep the general idea of the principle in mind.

3. 80/20-ing to Perfection

Another mistake made in applying the rule is linking it with skill-building. The misconception goes that it will take two years to become 80% proficient at one skill and another eight years to become fully proficient. While this might sound like a useful application of the rule, it goes against the concept. You are still doing 100% to fully master the skill instead of focusing on the first 20%. The point is that the 80/20 rule is not particularly useful in the realms of skill-building.

4. Still Focusing on the 80%

After all the analysis and classification you have done, you might still feel the need to go for the 80%. After all, these are a bigger group of tasks, and getting them done could give you an illusion that you have achieved a lot. Indeed, the 80% still needs to be done, but not necessarily by you, or as the highest priority, or with the most outstanding level of details and perfection. Implementing the 80/20 principle requires a change in your mindset. It would be best if you accepted that the relationship between the inputs (i.e., the tasks) and the outputs (i.e., the impact on reaching the intended goals) is not one to one. In other words, the tasks in the 80% category do not generate 80% of the results. You can always decide to focus on getting the 80% perfect. But remember that you will not achieve more than 20% of the desired results.

Implementing the 80/20 principle does not mean ignoring the 80%. As discussed before, the 80% should be handled properly handled. Any trivial task with little contribution to achieving the desired goals should be skipped or minimized. Delegation should be used as much as possible. The remaining tasks should be done according to their priority.

To summarize:

The 80/20 rule is highly compatible with the concept of Productivity. After all, you tend to get things done faster if you know which of your activities contribute to your success the most. Please keep in mind that the 80/20 principle is merely a guideline. What matters is the principle's core concept, that the relationship between our efforts and what we achieve is not linear. This imbalance could be used to get more done with the same amount of time and effort or achieve the desired result with less of those precious resources. The whole process starts with identifying activities that bring the most value to your life. Those activities should then be prioritized, nurtured, and multiplied.

CHAPTER VIII

BETTER DONE THAN PERFECT

"The perfect is the enemy of the good."

Voltaire

Do not get the wrong idea; there is nothing wrong with getting things done with perfection. Excelling at something is always to be admired as it sets the standard. After all, without standards, concepts like productivity and success would not exist at all. However, such a drive for excellence could also hinder you from getting started with various tasks. Similarly, the compulsion to be flawless, precise, and graceful can put a severe toll on your mind, body, and personal and professional development.

In Chapter 5, we discussed how perfectionism could become a productivity killer. Now, the question is what we can do about our tendency to get things done with perfection and reconcile such a desire with high productivity. Being a perfectionist is not a negative attribute on its own. On the contrary, it could be precious if it is used wisely and timely. This chapter will build on the learnings from Chapters 6 and 7 about developing habits and using the 80/20 principle and will discuss how to embrace imperfection in our daily life while occasionally leveraging our perfectionist attitude only when it is genuinely needed.

Adjusting the Perfectionist Mindset

To address perfectionism, you have to remember that this mindset has roots in your self-worth. In essence, whatever worth you assign to yourself will determine the quality level you deem acceptable. The fear of not meeting the standards set by yourself or by others can prevent you from starting a task in the first place because not meeting those standards can lower your sense of self-worth. Adjusting this mindset starts with breaking the link between doing something perfectly and your self-worth. In the following section, we will discuss five tips on developing a new mindset with a different approach towards perfectionism.

1. Use Self-Criticism for Growth

The controlling emotion in perfectionism is the fear of not living up to the standards. For a perfectionist, these standards are usually self-imposed. Combine this fear with the severe blow to one's ego with any actual or presumed failure, and you have a rather potent source of procrastination. Being self-critical could help us grow and achieve more. But being self-critical with a growth mindset is constructive while beating yourself because you did not meet very high and sometimes unrealistic standards is destructive. If you set a particular goal and do your best to achieve it, you have done a great job and could do even better the next time. This is the growth mindset and is totally different from a black and white and rigid perfectionism where you are either the best or a complete failure.

2. Break the Link Between Performance and Self-Worth

It feels good to win, meet a deadline, go beyond expectations, reach the targets, and so on. But how do you handle failure, reaching a part of your targets, not being perfect? Everyone fails from time to time, even if they try their best. For every winner, there are many losers. This is just a normal part of our lives. Interpreting the failures or imperfections as your incapability or lack of intelligence is a genuinely self-sabotaging behavior.

How you deal with setbacks plays a vital role in what you make out of your life. The worst you can do is to link them to your self-worth. Just keep in mind that you can fail, but you are not a failure. Most successful people in any field have had to deal with many setbacks in their lives. Take Abraham Lincoln as an example. Between 1832 when he ran for Illinois House of Representatives for the first time, and 1860 when he became the 16th US President, Lincoln had all sorts of failure or setbacks, from losing loved ones to a nervous breakdown and losing his job to losing elections multiple times. After almost every setback, he came on the top with a new success, got re-elected, and continued until he won the Presidential elections in 1860. The life of Abraham Lincoln is a brilliant example of the growth mindset. Had he interpreted every failure as an indication of his inability as a person, he would have never been able to bounce back, overcome the setbacks, and use them to pave the way toward future success.

3. Do Away with the Blank Slate

For perfectionists, everything matters and everything has to be done right the first time. Take writing a book as an example. If you are writing a book, you might have difficulty writing the introduction, perhaps because you cannot think of the "best" choice of words to start everything. So, instead of just getting started and review and edit later, you keep staring at the blank slate looking for the perfect words! But here's the secret that most writers know: the first draft is rarely the best. Once everything is written, the next and more intensive phase would be editing, re-phrasing, restructuring, and revising the entire text. Sometimes, your first draft would be totally ripped apart and built up again.

The blank slate cannot be edited. There is no way to reach perfection if that thing remains to be created. By not trying to make things perfect, you increase your chances of getting things done. There is always room for improvement once you have a draft or at least a concept.

4. Manage Your Standards

The problem with perfectionism is that it can twist the acceptable level of output. What is "okay" for the perfectionists is most probably "really good" for everybody else. So, doing a reality check might help with adjusting your expectations. Not every task requires the same level of meticulousness or flawlessness. What you have to give should be proportionate to what the task requires. There is no need to overdo things if the requirements have already been met. Also, realize that what the rest of the world needs is "good enough" in many cases. Ask yourself this: what is more important to your superiors, teammates, and co-workers that you do the task perfectly or timely and with acceptable quality? This is not a call for mediocrity but a reminder that less than perfect quality is just fine in most instances.

5. The 80/20 Principle Is Your Best Friend

We talked about the 80/20 principle in the previous chapter. This principle's core concept is the imbalance between the inputs and their impact on the output. Perhaps you find the advice to let go of perfectionism altogether too radical. If that is the case, then try to 80/20 your desire for perfectionism. In other words, choose your 20% vital tasks and get them done perfectly. For the other 80%, try to forget perfectionism. In this way, you can still get the satisfaction of delivering flawless results when it matters the most without strangling yourself with the compulsion of getting everything perfect.

As mentioned in the previous chapter, perfectionism and the 80/20 principle are not compatible. It does not make sense to get 80% of the tasks perfect because they will not contribute more than 20% to the overall result. If the desire to achieve impeccable results is limited to the vital 20%, it could be a very constructive force. But it has to be compensated by lowering the expectations on the other 80% of the tasks.

Embracing Imperfections

If you think about it, perfectionism is just a fear of producing something that may not live to your standards. It is that need to always create something extraordinary and groundbreaking. Do not get the wrong idea. Learning to embrace imperfection is not the same as mediocrity. You still have to give your best, but you should also accept that not every outcome will be perfect regardless of how you put effort into it. What is important is that you make the first step towards creating something of value instead of keeping that idea locked away behind some unrealistic standard. To embrace the concept of imperfection, first, you have to get comfortable with the idea that not everything has to be perfect. This does not need to happen in one massive leap from excellence to sloppiness. It starts with adjusting unreasonable standards to something entirely within your ability to reach consistently. It is from

"Perfect" to "Good Enough", from "Excellent" to "Meets Standards".

For example, imagine you want to write a new book about improving productivity. You might be tempted to include every possible subject or theory involved with the topic and create the most comprehensive source of enhancing productivity. Similarly, you might want to make sure that all your information will remain evergreen. But if you think about it, not every book covering one topic can include every possible talking point on that subject. Information will eventually become outdated, and new topics relevant to the subject matter will regularly pop up. This is why every book has an "edition" to give the author a chance to update their work as they see fit. A more realistic approach for you as the author would be to do your best and create the book's first edition knowing that the first edition will never remain timeless, no matter how good it is. The same line of thinking applies in every aspect of personal or professional life. When you want to learn a new hobby, start a new relationship, find a new school for your kid, or develop a new product, write a report, form a new team, and so on, you will face the same challenge. In other words, you can either set realistic expectations, get started and do your best, or impose very high standards, stay paralyzed, and never start or complete anything. This act of setting the bar not too high lies at the heart of embracing imperfection.

So far, we have talked about how to adjust the perfectionist mindset and how to start embracing imperfections. With this change in perspective, you should be ready for some practical tips on implementing a new attitude. Here are nine tips on leveraging your desire for excellence when it makes a difference while embracing imperfection most of the time.

1. Learn to "Satisfice"

Yes, that is an actual word! The term "Satisfice" is a combination of "satisfy" and "suffice" and was coined in 1956 by the economist Herbert A. Simon to explain the decision-making process. When we want to decide, we would ideally gather all the relevant information, identify all possible solutions, and choose the best solution after comparing them all. Simon explained that most often, we have to make decisions under conditions such as little time, incomplete information, and without being able to determine the best possible solution. Hence, we choose the first reasonable solution, check if we cannot find significant issues with it, and we move on.

Perfectionists tend to overdo things. They like to maximize, i.e., they want to achieve the best, the most effective and flawless solutions, beat the expectations, over-deliver, and meet the highest standards. For them, everything deserves the maximum effort, while in practice, most tasks could be done with a fraction of that effort.

Embracing imperfection is transforming from a maximizer to a satisficer, from yearning for perfection to being content with the good enough. The goal is to not shoot way over the target but to hit it with the right amount of time and effort. A satisficer knows that there is no perfect decision and no perfectly executed plan. As such, they seek the decision that hits most of their objectives and needs. By learning satisficing instead of maximizing, you tend to make more effective decisions faster. After all, it is quicker to develop a realistic course of action than the best possible course in every scenario.

The ideas of Herbert Simon were remarkably similar to those formulated in the 80/20 principle. He believed in spending "enough" time and energy on making a particular decision, and how much that "enough" is, depends on the criticality of the decision. Satisficing in decision-making is similar to the 80/20 principle for completing various tasks. If a task belongs to your 80% of non-vital tasks, it contributes to only 20% of the results. Hence, it would be sufficient to get that task done quickly while meeting the necessary standards. Productivity could be enhanced by satisficing for 80% of the tasks and then dedicating more time and energy to other 20% vital tasks. This will allow you to prevent decision-fatigue, increase efficiency, decrease stress, and eventually boost your productivity.

If you tend to understand satisficing as the opposite of optimizing (and not the opposite of maximizing), you can still use it for the 80% non-vital tasks. What matters is the core message of the satisficing concept; that you should aim at good-enough results in most cases. In this way, you will at least save yourself from spending the maximum time and effort in 80% of the cases and focus on trying to get the 20% vital tasks in an optimum way.

2. Do Not Fall Prey to Analysis Paralysis

Perfectionists do not deal with one winning idea. They entertain a lot simultaneously and could end up paralyzed, not knowing where and how to start. In most cases, you do not know which concept will yield the best result or which one fits your current needs. Regardless, you are stuck trying to choose one good idea from the rest. As we discussed before on the decision-making process, maximizers would like to know all possible solutions for a problem, their pros and cons, and decide only after a thorough comparison. In ideal conditions, such an approach increases the chances of making the best decision. However, as mentioned by Herbert Simon, real-world situations usually involve incomplete information and limited time. Trying to overthink and overanalyze everything will result in not being able to decide at all.

This state of being paralyzed by analyzing too much is a typical manifestation of perfectionist tendency. Perfectionists want to make sure that whatever idea they choose will be the best. They hate being wrong, and they like to show to themselves and others that they can deliver the highest quality results. This falls back again to their self-worth being connected to the output that they create.

The desire to do due diligence is fine. But it can kill your productivity if it results in paralysis by analysis. You can use the 80/20 principle and the concept of satisficing to address paralysis by analysis effectively. If you keep in mind that in general 80% of the tasks contribute to only 20% of your overall output, you can satisfice with them, get them done with a good-enough quality, and avoid overthinking or overanalyzing. In this way, you will have more time and energy to focus on the vital 20% of the tasks.

3. Go Beyond Impressions

In most cases, our idea of perfection is merely aesthetic. It is all those elaborations that we put on the output. In simpler terms, our view of perfection is mostly skin deep. But it is on those needless elaborations that we spend a lot of our mental energies. Again, using the book-writing analogy, we might spend a lot of time worrying about the inconveniences that are the easiest to fix when we should be focusing on meeting the base objectives. Did you use "you're" instead of "you are"? Is the page numbering in the middle of the page or on the corner? Did you use the best-looking fonts? Such a level of attention to detail might sometimes be needed. But for a large majority of cases, it will just prevent you from delivering the goods on time. The truth is most people value utility more than aesthetics. Sometimes they go hand in hand, but if an average Joe has to pick one over another, he would most probably go with something useful rather than something pretty.

4. Time is Precious

Perfectionism does not prevent a person from delivering quality. It prevents them from providing that quality *on time*. After all, they spend a lot of time creating the perfect condition to start the task, tend to overanalyze and overdo it, and are uncomfortable with delivering anything slightly imperfect. Thus, one of the biggest challenges that perfectionists have to clear is their ability to work within the available time for a particular task. That endless nitpicking and tweaking could prevent them from finishing tasks on time. Planning will be the key here; it will give you an idea of when to start on a task, when to deliver it, and when to start the next item. This becomes even more essential when working in teams and on bigger or more complicated projects.

Think of time as a finite resource. Our daily lives are full of time-limited tasks; the kid has to be at school at a specific time, bills have to be paid in time, work projects have deadlines, and so on. Time is precious, and it should be allotted appropriately. An effective way to boost your productivity is to prioritize your time and complete the tasks according to how much time you assigned to them. For example, you can quickly complete trivial tasks to spend more time on the more important ones. The opposite strategy could also be used; you can finish the vital 20% of the tasks first and spend the remaining time on the trivial 80%.

5. Don't Wait for Perfect Conditions

We all had that teacher who would brusquely tell everyone in the class to "Come to my class prepared or don't come at all!". Sadly, many take this threat to heart. The danger of being discovered to be ill-prepared for a lesson often causes some students to not come to class at all. This is something not limited to classroom settings. Many of us think to start losing weight, learning new skills, beginning with the next projects, getting a new hobby, sharing a product concept, and so on, we need perfect conditions. Perfectionism breeds procrastination. We keep postponing our plans to a future time when "perfect" conditions will be present. But what if those conditions never happen? The truth is for the vast majority of tasks, it is better to simply get into action and use the momentum created to take more steps. Certain decisions require more due diligence. For some, it could be starting a family, for others, maybe buying a house or moving to another city to take a new job. But even for those decisions, you have to act after a reasonable time. The need to have perfect conditions before getting started is also a manifestation of procrastination, an excuse not to start with the intended task.

Starting without having the perfect conditions in place will make perfectionists uncomfortable. It is unrealistic to assume that we will create our imaginary perfect conditions for every task we want to start. Hence, it is not possible to remove that feeling of discomfort. The key to getting started is to learn to live with that discomfort and not to remove it. This can happen over time and with some practice. You can begin with one of the trivial tasks; make a quick plan for it, and get started. Once the task is completed, you are one step closer to embracing imperfection and its accompanying discomfort.

6. Define the Task Using an Outline

You could also work out your tendency to nitpick by defining the task's overall scope in an outline. This method is useful for bigger tasks involving multiple sub-tasks and is very common in workplaces. Defining an outline or a project plan allows you to describe the expected outcome, explore the possible ways to reach the intended goal, and define various project stages. You can include the available time and resources in the outline and get an idea of how much time and energy is needed to complete that task. Setting your expectation for each part of the task could prevent you from overthinking and overdoing. If you can stay committed to the outline and the plan, you will force yourself to give up the perfectionist tendencies.

As long as outlining does not become a new project of its own, you can use this strategy for all sorts of tasks, at work or home, for large or small projects. The level of detail in an outline depends on the complexity and the size of the intended task. A daily to-do list combined with a brief outline for the vital tasks could be a good starting point.

7. Judge Yourself as You Judge Your Best Friend

Your inner critical voice tends to be the loudest when you create something. As such, your goal at this phase would be to make it shut up. A psychological test you could run on yourself is what is called the Best Friend test. Imagine that somebody got a 99% or an A++ on a recent exam. Now, imagine that person to be you, and you were aiming for 100%. What would you say to yourself, knowing that you were one point shy of perfection? Use the same figure. But this time, the person that got the 99% was a friend of yours. What would you say to your best friend who may, for the first time, actually got the highest marks for that test? More often than not, you will criticize yourself for not living up to your standard while praising your friend who aced that test. This does give rise to the question: Why are you treating yourself differently? Similarly, when your best friend experiences a setback or makes a mistake, do you talk to him or her harshly, or do you try to be comforting and helpful? We tend to be too critical of ourselves. Maybe we think self-criticism will motivate us. But in most cases, it will result in increased distress and low mood.

An obsession for perfection causes harsh self-criticisms, lowers self-worth and performance, and prevents you from taking risks. Self-criticism could become a vehicle for growth if done correctly, i.e., constructively and focused on continuous improvement. You can focus on doing your best, and improving yourself incrementally instead of worrying about when you will be the best. As Mark Twain said, *"Continuous improvement is better than delayed perfection."*

8. Have Someone Hold You Accountable

We talked about managing your standards and defining the scope of tasks using outlines. Once you have taken these two steps, it is essential to hold yourself accountable for completing the intended task within the defined limits and standards. Accountability systems are not entirely new in the workplace, and they work on a relatively simple concept. Usually, your manager or team lead continuously monitors you and checks on your progress. He or she will continually prod you to do tasks on time and give reminders here and there. This could be more challenging in personal life where self-discipline is the primary tool to hold ourselves accountable.

Accountability is a counterbalance against perfectionism. You can hold yourself accountable or ask your boss or a colleague to do it for you. Having an accountability coach or partner could prevent you from creeping back to your perfectionist tendencies. What is ingenious about this is that it takes advantage of a perfectionist's tendency to self-criticize. Your accountability partner can help you along the way until you build a habit of holding yourself accountable to the set targets.

9. Use Self-Talk to Tune Out Perfectionism

Most of us practice self-talk regularly. Sometimes it is to motivate ourselves, other times to evaluate or instruct. Research shows that self-talk can effectively enhance our performance and boost our productivity. Motivational self-talk could psyche us up for a challenging task. Considering past events and helping ourselves to learn new skills or perform complex tasks are the other areas where self-talk could be useful.

You can use a combination of all three self-talk strategies mentioned above to address your negative thoughts. For example, a list of the usual thoughts you might entertain while working on a work project could include the following:

- This is too lame. Restart everything!
- This has been tried before. What's the point?
- Everything's crap anyway. Just drop what you're doing.

Effective self-talk usually involves using positive words and focusing on what you can achieve rather than what you should avoid. For example, the negative thoughts mentioned above could be refuted and reversed if you talk the following to yourself:

- Why don't I just finish everything first and edit afterward?
- Can I rephrase the entire concept, then?
- Finish this task ASAP and let the others judge the quality later.

With practice, you can effectively tune out your nitpicking tendencies. You can use the strategies discussed so far in this book in your self-talks; think of the 80/20 principle, satisficing, outlining, getting started instead of waiting for perfect conditions, focusing on utility rather than the looks, and so on.

To summarize:

Perfectionists have all-or-nothing thinking without many shades in between. They tend to set the bar very high and feel like a failure when they cannot meet those high standards. A combination of rigid thinking, sky-high standards, and self-criticism set perfectionists up for frustration, procrastination, giving up early, and lower productivity.

Changing your mindset and becoming comfortable with imperfection are vital here. In this chapter, we talked about how tools such as the 80/20 principle, satisficing, self-talk, constructive criticism, planning, accountability, and so on could help you bring your perfectionist tendencies under control. The truth is that one cannot entirely get rid of their perfectionism. If it is innate with your personality, it will stick with you for as long as you live. If you cannot get rid of that perfectionism, you could then learn to curb it, channel it constructively, and use it in a manner that aids your productivity. Instead of being obsessed with perfection, focus on continuous improvement, and doing your best to achieve sustained success and happiness.

CHAPTER IX

WALKING THE WORK-LIFE BALANCE TIGHTROPE

"Waiting is a trap. There will always be reasons to wait. The truth is, there are only two things in life, reasons and results, and reasons simply don't count."

Robert Anthony

I magine you have taken everything you read in this book by heart and have applied them gracefully. You are now enjoying great productivity and rarely experience procrastination. How do you envision that life? Are you earning more, finishing your to-do list every day, going to the gym more often, or maybe learning new hobbies and building new relationships? Perhaps everyone has a unique answer to this question. Can we find a common thread in all of the responses? This chapter tries to find that common thread. The goal is to put everything discussed so far into life's broader perspective and to see how we can apply the learnings into our everyday life.

So far, we have been talking about two main topics: beating procrastination and boosting productivity in personal and professional life. But what does all of this mean? Does it mean to try to achieve more and more? That sounds a bit perfectionist. How about working harder and longer? We want to be productive, not busy. So, working hard and long is also not the answer. The truth is bringing procrastination under control, and sustainably improving productivity require a holistic approach to work and life. We can follow the 80/20 principle to prioritize daily tasks at work or relationships in personal life, but we cannot say, "I will spend 80% of my time and energy on work and 20% on my private life", or vice versa. The ideas and concepts presented in this book have been discussed mainly in a single context, for example, at work. But in reality, different aspects of our lives are connected and compete for the limited resources of time, energy, money, etc. Hence, for effective implementation of what you have learned from this book, you should look at your life as a whole and not just one aspect of it. For example, if being very productive at work consumes all of your mental energy, you will become unhappy and not able to sustain that productivity.

Going back to the question posed at the beginning of this chapter, my vision of a life where I rarely procrastinate and enjoy high productivity at home and work is when I have a good work-life balance. The definition of work-life balance is a little different for everyone. That is not surprising as we have different priorities and circumstances. In this chapter, we will dive deeper into how to combine all the learnings of the previous chapters to achieve a good work-life balance to have sustained happiness and productivity.

What Work-Life Balance Is and Is Not

On September 6th, 1991, Brian Dyson, former CEO of Coca-Cola Enterprises, delivered the 172nd commencement speech at Georgia Tech. In a part of his speech, he presents his vision on what the most important in our lives are:

"Imagine life as a game in which you are juggling some five balls in the air. You name them - work, family, health, friends, and spirit - and you're keeping all of these in the air. You will soon understand that work is a rubber ball. If you drop it, it will bounce back. But the other four balls - family, health, friends, and spirit - are made of glass. If you drop one of these, they will be irrevocably scuffed, marked, nicked, damaged or even shattered. They will never be the same. You must understand that and strive for balance in your life."

Juggling balls is an excellent analogy for how we have to manage various aspects of our lives. In reality, life could be even more challenging because we have to keep juggling those five balls while moving toward our goals and going through the ups and downs of life. So, in fact, life could feel like juggling balls while walking on a tightrope, and you are the acrobat on the high wire! We can learn a lot from the acrobat on the tightrope. Here are some examples: there are no "perfect" conditions for the acrobat to cross the tightrope, he has to juggle the balls while keeping his balance, there is a lot of noise around him, some days he crosses the rope easier than in other days, he has to keep his focus and courage until reaching his goal, and so on.

For most of us, the feeling of contentment occurs when we have achieved our goals while enjoying the path to those goals. For example, if we like a college course, learn a lot from it and pass the course with a good mark, we will not feel overwhelmed or exhausted. Instead, we will have a feeling of fulfillment and satisfaction after completing that course. The same goes for finishing a project at work or learning a hobby. Perhaps you will get the same feelings of achievement and joy in an ordinary day if you can manage to get the work done reasonably well while still having the time and energy to enjoy your personal life. The two everyday concepts of achievement and joy are at the core of a healthy work-life balance. Achievement is reaching our goals, and joy encompasses the feeling of satisfaction and happiness. If you think about it, achievement and joy are what drive us and give our lives value. So, if we can achieve something at work and home every day and enjoy doing what we do, our life as a whole will be in balance.

Perhaps everyone agrees with the conceptual meaning of work-life balance, as discussed above. However, it gets more complicated when we try to come up with a more tangible and universally-agreeable definition because the "balance" is different for each of us. Your balance might include working from home or switching from full-time to part-time so that you can take care of your private life. It could be working even more for somebody else because that person might tremendously enjoy their job. In principle, trying to develop a one-size-fits-all definition for work-life balance is futile; there is no single definition here! The right balance would be different depending on whether you are single or have a few kids, what kind of job you do, what your preferences and priorities are, and so on. Even your right balance for today could be other than what you need tomorrow.

Work-life balance could not be a rigid or an idealized concept. Thinking of work-life balance as having an extremely productive day at work, leaving early to spend a fantastic afternoon and evening with friends and family is a perfectionist vision that rarely happens. It would be best to focus on a realistic and flexible schedule that allows you to plan each day according to your priorities. Some days you might focus more on work and others more on spending time with family. As long as you can achieve something meaningful and enjoy along the way, you will be in balance!

How Can the Balance Boost Your Productivity?

If you think about all the benefits of a healthy work-life balance, you will agree that trying to learn how to juggle the balls while walking on life's tightrope is worth it. Although some people might think work-life balance equals working less, getting less done, and having lower productivity, it is generally believed that a sufficient work-life balance improves our productivity. As mentioned before, work-life balance does not necessarily equal working fewer hours, and we also know that working more hours is not the same as getting more done. A healthy balance between work and personal life can improve our overall life quality and that, in turn, boosts our productivity. How could this happen? Let's review a few ways.

1. Reduced Stress Level

Our body produces cortisol to take action against stressors. Increased levels of cortisol in short bursts help us to get energized and act quickly. However, if stressors last for too long, our performance and productivity will significantly suffer from the chronically elevated cortisol levels. Higher stress levels could have professional or personal reasons, such as being overloaded at work or having family issues. A healthy work-life balance gives us the flexibility to focus on our priorities at a specific time. For example, that flexibility might allow us to work part-time, from home, or with flexible hours to take care of a loved one, which will reduce our stress and will enable us to cope with the situation better. A more balanced life will allow us to focus more on work when needed and be consistently more productive.

2. Lower Chances of Burn-out

The World Health Organization (WHO) officially recognizes chronic workplace stress, also known as burn-out, as a severe health issue. WHO defines burnout as follows:

"Burn-out is a syndrome conceptualized as resulting from chronic workplace stress that has not been successfully managed. It is characterized by three dimensions:

- *feelings of energy depletion or exhaustion;*

- *increased mental distance from one's job, or feelings of negativism or cynicism related to one's job; and*

- *reduced professional efficacy.*

Burn-out refers specifically to phenomena in the occupational context and should not be applied to describe experiences in other areas of life."

Burn-out is a major cause of lost productivity. According to WHO's definition, managing workplace stress is vital in preventing the occurrence of burn-out. Employers have an important role in creating an environment in which employees are not chronically stressed-out. Our focus here is on what we as individuals can do to manage stress at the workplace and in our personal life. Prioritization and setting clear goals can tremendously help with not being overworked. Furthermore, a balanced life that allows us to be flexible with our work and have some time and energy to enjoy life will help manage daily stresses. Aiming at being productive without paying enough attention to how we handle stress build-ups (both at work and home) might work in the short-term and is not sustainable.

3. Improved Motivation and Mental Health

Mental health is a crucial component to our overall well-being. Conditions such as depression and anxiety affect us as individuals and result in productivity loss. The WHO data shows that mental health issues are responsible for US$ 140 billion of lost productivity per year in the WHO European Region alone. Work aversion is a natural stress response so that the body does not repeatedly experience such negative emotions. Balance helps by letting you deal with stress more constructively. With your stress effectively dealt with, you will have an easier time performing tasks. Combine this with a sound incentive system, and you might even feel eager to take on challenges in your work.

4. Better outlook in life and work

A better work-life balance and all the benefits that come with it improve relationships with colleagues at work and with the loved ones at home. It increases employee engagement and the overall outlook in life and work. Whether as an employee or as a self-employed, a positive outlook, and being more motivated enhance productivity. For organizations, employee engagement and positive perception about work are critical to achieving high productivity and low employee turnover. When people feel included in and connected to their workplace, they are more willing to contribute to their workplace's overall goals; function more efficiently, are more enthusiastic about their jobs, and are psychologically and emotionally invested in their workplace. Organizations have a vital role in creating a positive outlook for their employees in general and a healthy work-life balance in particular. The truth is that when it comes to work-life balance, many factors are not under our control. What we are focused on here are those factors that are within our circles of control and influence.

Better Work-Life Balance for Higher Productivity

So far in this chapter, we have discussed what work-life balance is and what it is not and have also reviewed how it can boost productivity. It should be clear by now that having the flexibility to prioritize work or personal life as needed, not being overworked or stressed out, feelings of achievement and enjoyment in life, and so on will undoubtedly boost our productivity. The challenge would be how to reach such a balanced life and sustain that balance in everyday life.

Achieving a healthy balance between work life and personal life will call upon many of the concepts discussed so far in this book. The good news is that a healthy work-life balance and high productivity have a lot in common, and the same set of measures could improve them both. Many of the concepts and habits discussed in Chapters 6-8 to boost productivity are very relevant for improving work-life balance. There is a feedback loop between work-life balance and productivity. This feedback loop could be both positive and negative, i.e., they can amplify or damper each other. Furthermore, a healthy work-life balance could not be maintained without developing good habits, which is similar to creating habits to sustain high productivity.

In this section, we will revisit some of the previously-discussed ideas in the context of work-life balance. This could also help clarify the feedback loops between balance and productivity. We will also discuss seven new ideas on creating and maintaining the balance for sustained success and productivity.

1. Use Available Options to Improve the Balance

Let's start with an apparent item. If your organization offers any measures which could help you achieve a better work-life balance, use them. Flexible working hours, working from home, extra leave days, childcare assistance, employee assistance, counseling programs, gym membership, occupational health services, and so on. Do your research and find out what options are available for you. You might be able to get support from family or friends for some personal responsibilities. Using all available options is like low hanging fruit and could become the starting point to improve your work-life balance.

2. Apply What You Have Learned in This Book!

We have discussed many concepts and strategies in this book to help you bring procrastination under control and boost your productivity. The feedback loops between productivity and work-life balance would mean that many of those strategies and concepts could directly or indirectly enhance work-life balance. Habits or practices that can help you work more efficiently, get more done, or reach the targets sooner and with less effort could be applied in personal and professional lives. Let's review some habits and strategies that can help you bring better harmony between your work life and personal life.

Suppose you are someone who continually deals with a lot of commitments or is a full-time employee. Then juggling different responsibilities and problems is going to be a daily occurrence. There are always demands to be satisfied at home, school, work, or with friends and neighbors, deadlines to be met, and problems to be solved or delegated. Then, there are those days where it is nearly impossible to focus on one without letting others go. You see in this description (and perhaps you know from experience) that real-life situations are often chaotic, dynamic, and unpredictable. Anything you have learned in this book should be applied against the backdrop of our busy and ever-changing daily lives.

Time is a precious and limited resource. This becomes very clear when you try to get things done while achieving harmony between your work and private life. It is essential to identify, eliminate, or at least limit your time-wasters at work and home. Start by taking note of how you spend your day. Whether it is too many random chats with colleagues at work, watching TV a few hours every day, social media, YouTube videos, or anything else, there is always some time to be saved and used more productively. Nowadays, many people spend a substantial amount of time in meetings, either in person or online. Maybe you can shorten some meetings and replace a few others with sending an email. Prioritization, delegation, deep work, and satisficing could be used to get things done faster and without sacrificing overall output quality.

We usually know most of the items on our to-do list in advance. A great habit to improve work-life balance is to plan for such things. For example, before the day ends, you can give your mind a head start and plan what to do the next day. It will also help if you can set boundaries between your personal and professional to-do list, meaning you do not keep working in your free time and focus on work during working hours.

Your ability to regulate the amount of effort and focus you will give in each task is another critical factor. As we discussed in Chapters 6 and 7, not all tasks require the same effort. A high priority task, like an important work project or term paper, will require 100% of your focus and effort. However, more straightforward tasks like filing regular reports or answering most emails could be done with a good-enough quality or delegated.

Do not forget to be flexible and improvise as needed. Aiming at rigid plans, always being in control, and beating yourself up if things do not go as planned does not help to bring balance to your life. You know your life, your strength, and your limitations better than anybody else. You can seek help and advice, but in the end, it is your life. You can decide on what your priorities are and how to focus on them. So, use these learnings and adapt them to your unique circumstances.

3. Take Care of Yourself

Warren Buffet, one of the most successful investors of all times, shares an intriguing story in his biography *The Snowball: Warren Buffett and the Business of Life*, where he tries to explain the importance of taking care of yourself to a group of students. In his story, a genie appears to the 16-year-old Warren and offers him a car of his choice. Warren is smart enough to know that there should be a catch, and he is right. The genie tells him that this will be his last car and it has to last a lifetime. Buffet then says if he takes the car, he will read the owner's manual a few times before driving it, always garages it, protects and maintains it so well that it lasts a lifetime. He uses this analogy to talk about two things that we cannot neglect in life: our body and mind. Buffet continues his story as follows:

> *"You only get one mind and one body. And it's got to last a lifetime. But if you don't take care of that mind and that body, they'll be a wreck 40 years later...it's what you do right now, today, that determines how your mind and body will operate 10, 20, and 30 years from now."*

Achieving work-life balance and maintaining it would not be possible without taking care of your mind and body. Meditation, reflection, and meaningful relationships could help with protecting your mind. Try to include some time for yourself in your must-do list. During that time, what you do is entirely up to you; it could be exercising, attending a therapy session, doing charitable work, watching a movie, or whatever that gives you joy and helps you relieve stress. A healthy lifestyle, including enough sleep and exercise, will refresh both mind and body. Remember, you have just one mind and one body. Healthy work-life balance, productivity, success, or any other goal could not be achieved or sustained without taking care of yourself!

4. Focus on Efficiency

If productivity is getting things done, efficiency is how much resource is consumed to get those things done; the less time and effort used to complete a task, the higher the efficiency. The essential resource to enhance work-life balance is time. Assuming that the to-do list and the priority of the tasks in the list are set, you should focus on getting them done with the highest efficiency. In many real-world situations, the list of tasks is not fixed; a new project is given to you on short notice, you get unanticipated family duties, your car or fridge breaks down and needs repair, etc. High efficiency means you can get more tasks done within a fixed amount of time, without the need for overwork, continue working from home or at the weekends.

Many of the techniques discussed in Chapters 6-8 could be used to increase efficiency. Deep work, the Eisenhower model, satisficing, and planning are some examples. If you know your to-do list, you can plan and prioritize them in advance and get them done faster using deep work, as discussed in Chapter 6. The same approach could be used for unanticipated tasks, except that deciding on the urgency and importance of the task should be done on the spot. In either case, you can use satisficing and the 80/20 rule to decide on the output's acceptable quality. The last point is critical in avoiding perfectionism and achieving high efficiency.

5. Do Not Aim at a "Perfect" Work-Life Balance

In previous chapters, we talked in detail about perfectionism, how it can damage your productivity, and how important it is to embrace imperfection. Such a mindset applies to productivity and many other aspects of life, including work-life balance. Suppose you imagine work-life balance as going home early after a highly productive workday and spending a fantastic evening with family and friends. In that case, you are setting your expectations so unrealistically high that you will be disappointed most of the days. Soon you will believe that achieving work-life balance is a myth and give up your efforts altogether.

Instead of aiming at perfection with your work-life balance, strive for continuous improvements and realistic targets. As discussed earlier in this chapter, there is no perfect work-life balance. The balance is not constant; some days you need more time for work, other days you should spend more time and attention on the family. In reality, life is fluid and unpredictable. Any plan to improve work-life balance should be adaptable, incremental, having realistic goals, and with some room for improvisations.

6. Survive the Crunch Times

Regardless of your work field, there are always periods wherein everybody has to work longer, produce more, and deal with more stress head-on. Such crunch times might include meeting a crucial departmental goal, completing work before the holidays, or something as simple as an overbooked work calendar. Crunch times are unavoidable in most work environments. As such, the best thing to do is to prepare yourself for them.

First of all, do not waste precious mental energies complaining about the situation. Instead, focus on planning for the upcoming wave of stress. Proper communication with your manager and colleagues becomes even more critical during crunch times. This could help set priorities, divide the workload, and support each other so that everybody can play to their strengths and get the job done as a team. You might also have to renegotiate less critical deadlines with your superiors or and adjust some plans.

During crunch periods, the balance leans towards work. You have to plan your personal duties around the working hours. Keeping your family informed about the situation will help them to understand that you need to focus on your work in the upcoming period.

You might have personal crunch times from time to time. The same principles as explained for crunch times at work apply here; talk to family and friends, get help if possible, inform your manager and teammates about your situation, plan and prioritize, and so on. Crunch times push our work-life balance to extremes. But with some resilience and adequate preparation, all of us can survive them.

7. Do What You Love or Make What You Do More Loveable

All of the previous measures assume that you do not hate your job or deeply dread starting a new workday. If your job continually drains your energy, something is wrong. Doing what you feel passionate about might sound a bit cliché, but it is very true for being productive and having a healthy work-life balance. The ideal situation is that you love what you do. In that case, working gives you energy and pleasure and automatically improves your overall well-being. When the exact opposite happens, i.e., you hate your job, your days will become uphill struggles. If your workplace has a toxic culture or is being run by toxic management, do yourself a favor and find another job!

For most people, some aspects of their job might be unpleasant or stressful. But if the job is, in general, interesting and fulfilling, there will be room for improvement. Perhaps you can talk to your manager and give some suggestions on how you can get your work done with a better work-life balance for you. It would be best to come up with some practical solutions based on your function and position. If you suggest to your manager that you can get the job done while working with flexible hours or partly from home, maybe you get what you want. Try not to moan or nag! Behaving professionally and coming up with solutions makes you more credible and gives you a better chance of succeeding.

To summarize:

Work-life balance could mean different things to different people. That is not surprising as we all have our preferences and priorities. For any one of us, the balance will be different in various life phases or even every day. This chapter discussed what work-life balance is and what it is not and reviewed several ideas to improve it. Better work-life balance can improve productivity in various ways.

Similarly, higher productivity usually leads to a better work-life balance. The opposite is also true, of course. The positive feedback loop between work-life balance and productivity means that both could be enhanced using the same set of measures. Obtaining work-life balance is a manifestation of many of the concepts discussed in this book. Suppose someone has clear priorities, focuses on the vital tasks, works efficiently, has mastered the art of satisficing, embraces imperfection, and is flexible and pragmatic enough. In that case, the chances are high that person is already enjoying a healthy work-life balance.

CHAPTER X

MAINTAINING AND TWEAKING YOUR PROGRESS

"Sow an act and you reap a habit. Sow a habit and you reap a character."

Charles Reade

From Procrastination to Productivity

Transforming yourself from a procrastinator to a highly productive person is like giving up some old habits and creating new ones. It will take time, effort, patience, and perseverance. It pushes you out of your comfort zone and challenges your determination. Old habits have a sticky nature; they are tenacious and hard to change. Once formed, it is challenging to get rid of them, even if we know they are harmful. A comic example of how sticky habits are, happened in a press conference in 1954 when UK Health Minister Iain Macleod shared the results of a study on smoking's harmful effects. He said the following while he and most of the reporters in the meeting room famously chain-smoked during the conference:

> *"It must be regarded as established that there is a relationship between smoking and cancer of the lung,"*

Habits dominate our lives, even if we are not fully aware of them. They form to help us do things with less effort. Without habits, we have to pay 100% attention to every task. Doing something habitually is like going on autopilot; we keep going without being fully conscious of what we do. You might have experienced this for your procrastination when you carry out trivial tasks to avoid more important ones as if you are unaware of the time or the consequences. The same is true for unproductiveness when we keep ourselves busy without delivering much output at the end of the day.

In previous chapters, we talked about many tools and strategies to transform yourself from a procrastinator to a productive person. These tools will provide you with a solid foundation to gradually build your new habits. However, you will face resistance along the way due to the sticky nature of procrastination and unproductiveness. This resistance will originate from your mind and also from the setbacks thrown to us in everyday life. Convincing yourself to stop checking social media updates and go back to work is hard. Concentrating, saying no to some request, and curbing your perfectionist tendencies are also hard. In your journey towards higher productivity and better work-life balance, you have to deal with the resistance within your mind while walking on the tightrope of life and joggling all the balls. You need some help to keep the balance on that rope.

What if walking on the rope on focusing on the joggling balls become your second nature? You will become like a skillful acrobat that walks on the rope every day with no sweat! Beating procrastination and boosting productivity should be engrained in your brains. Over time, you should able to do them as gracefully and habitually as an acrobat on the rope.

This last chapter of the book will focus on internalizing the previous chapters' learnings. The main goal is to help you sustain and strengthen your new habits when you face setbacks in real-life situations. You already know about the tools and concepts to stop procrastination and improve productivity. This chapter will discuss having the right mindset, realistic view on change, and the perseverance and hardiness to create productivity habits.

Building Productivity Habits

The process of creating a new habit is explained masterfully by Charles Duhigg in his book *"The Power of Habit"*, where he talks about the "habit loop". He explains this loop as follows:

> *"This process within our brains is a three-step loop. First, there is a cue, a trigger that tells your brain to go into automatic mode and which habit to use. Then there is the routine, which can be physical or mental or emotional. Finally, there is a reward, which helps your brain figure out if this particular loop is worth remembering for the future."*

So, to form new productivity habits, we should focus on the following three points:

- How to trigger the habit
- How to create a routine
- How to reward ourselves

You can start by identifying the triggers for your procrastination and unproductiveness. Perhaps removing them would be enough to set a more favorable course of action. Or maybe listening to an inspirational podcast or reminding yourself about your targets motivates you to stop procrastinating and getting into action.

The routine is basically repetition. In the same way that with enough practice, driving a car or riding a bicycle becomes habitual actions. You can perform them without much thinking. Following productivity routines make those routines a lot easier to implement.

The third element of the loop is rewarding yourself. You can do that incrementally and with any tangible progress towards your end goal. How to gratify yourself is up to you; maybe only the pleasant feeling of achievement is enough, or perhaps you need something a bit more tangible! The positive reinforcement created by rewarding makes it easier to go further. The loop can go on until you are satisfied with your newly-formed habit or maybe even further on.

Perseverance Is Key

Building any new habit needs practice and perseverance. Just like setting targets and standards, avoiding perfectionism is essential here. If you expect to finish this book (or any other book for that matter!) and tomorrow, you will miraculously transform into a productive go-getter, you will be disappointed. In the same way that you cannot learn to play the piano in a day or get six-pack abs in a week, you won't be able to change your habits overnight.

Instead, it would be best to consider your transformation as a journey and set your pace and expectations accordingly. You can start by taking small steps and, over time, get better. For example, if you know that you will procrastinate on any large or complicated project, you can start with the project's more straightforward or trivial tasks. Pushing yourself to begin with the most demanding tasks immediately requires a lot of willpower. If you do not see that willpower in yourself, do not give up. Doing more straightforward tasks first will contribute to the overall project while allowing you to get ready for the more challenging tasks.

Perseverance is also critical to face setbacks. The path to forming productivity habits will undoubtedly be full of setbacks. Most of these setbacks are out of your control. The question is, how you will react to them. You can either bounce back and surpass the setback or give up and stay where you are. Bouncing back after every failure separates the achievers from the losers. In chapter 8, we talked about how Abraham Lincoln faced so much adversity in his life and how he bounced back every time. Having a realistic vision and enough perseverance are among the most critical ingredients of your transformation towards becoming more productive.

Correction the Course as Needed

Did you know that Apollo 13 mission had seven course corrections before the mission was completed? So, despite all the accurate calculations and preparations, NASA scientists, engineers, and astronauts had to adjust the path multiple times to fulfill the mission. Just like the Apollo mission, your target is well known; you want to stop procrastinating, boost your productivity, and enhance your work-life balance in a sustained way. With eyes on these targets and your learnings and experiences, you start your journey. But because this journey's path is not crystal clear, you will need to correct your course from time to time. Learning from mistakes or experiences or merely following another route to your targets are all parts of the transformation. Having the flexibility to adjust as necessary to stay on course prevents you from hitting dead-ends and giving up on reaching your targets.

Focus on The Process Rather Than the Goal

Creating productivity habits is like running a marathon. You cannot run a marathon without consistent and proper training for quite some time. It takes time, effort, hardiness, and patience to run a marathon. Once you are in the race, you have to keep going for about two hours. You have to control your pace, be present, and keep your focus. Most people running a marathon are not doing it to win a race; they compete against themselves. They want to prove they can finish the race or maybe set a better personal record.

You cannot develop good habits just by fixating on the end goal. You have to focus on the process to reach that goal. You should establish the rituals, practice them regularly, and every time go a step further. In the same way that you cannot wake up one morning and decide to run a marathon, you won't be able to get rid of your procrastination tendencies overnight and transform into a productive person. Sustainable change is doable, but it takes time.

To summarize:

The previous chapters provide you with many tools and techniques to curb procrastination and boost productivity with the end goal of achieving a healthy work-life balance. This chapter tried to give you the right mindset and approach to form productivity habits that last. This chapter's main message was that real change happens over time and through perseverance, patience, and practice. Remember that a procrastinator's transformation to a productive person is like running a marathon and not running a sprint!

Closing Remarks

Compliments to you for making it so far! Hopefully, you enjoyed the book and learned from it. Perhaps you are wondering how and when to start implementing the ideas you learned here.

To answer that question, let's take a step back and think about why you choose this book in the first place. As mentioned in the introduction, this book is about getting started with an intended task or goal and getting it done efficiently. It tries to explain how to get things done by overcoming procrastination and boosting productivity. You probably wanted to learn more about how to transform yourself from a procrastinator to a producer. If we describe that transformation to climbing a massive rock (let's say 100 feet high), how would you start with the climb? How could you increase the chances that you will make it to the top?

Perhaps you will start by gathering the required tools such as the climbing rope, helmet, shoes, harness, etc. What you have learned from this book could be your tools for the climb. You are already well-equipped, and with some practice, you can use the tools skillfully. To have a higher chance of reaching the top, you need to take a few more steps. Here are four examples:

1. Set a Goal

In the rock-climbing analogy, the target is clear. How about your target? The transformation from a procrastinator to a highly productive person is a worthy goal, but it is also slightly vague. For example, do you like to have a clear to-do list every day and finish it off before going home (or around a specific time if you work from home)? Or perhaps you want to get your work done in four days per week and spend more time on your hobbies or with your family. Maybe you have your own business and would like to have more sales and more customers without working a lot more. The goal will very much depend on you and your situation.

In any case, try to set a clear target for your transformation. An alternative is to set intermediate targets and decide about the next step as you climb. For example, you might start by embracing imperfection while doing your favorite hobby or playing your favorite game.

Once you feel comfortable with imperfection, you do the same at work with more trivial tasks, then with more important projects, and so on. It is also up to you how ambitious you would like to be in setting your goals. You can start with more straightforward and safer goals and use the momentum to take up bigger and bolder goals afterward.

2. Make a Plan to Reach Your Goal

Depending on your experience, level of fitness, available time, weather conditions, etc., you might choose a different route to climb the rock. Your climbing partner might choose another route. Your path to reach the goal is specific to you, and you should plan for it accordingly. Probably you will check the rock to see which crack or ledge to use and plan your route accordingly. You know your skills and limitations, so you can plan your way to reach the target use your skills and strength while accepting or avoiding the limitations.

3. Make the First Move

Do not stay in the planning loop forever. Once you have set a target and a plan to reach it, take the first step. The fear of failure is normal, and it gets smaller as you move forward. Perhaps you have a fear of falling during the climb. But you know that you have made a plan and you are well-equipped. So, the chances of falling are meager. Because of the positive feedback loop between productivity and work-life balance, every step's success makes the next one easier to take. You will never know if the plan will work if you do not act. Even if the outcome is not entirely satisfactory, you learn something and do it better the next time.

4. Be Flexible

During the climb, you might need to change your route from time to time. The same is valid for creating productivity habits. To keep the juggling balls in the air, you have to be flexible and adjust as you go. Adaptability is crucial to deal with setbacks and ever-changing situations in everyday life. Your plans should not be too rigid with no room for compromises. You should also not beat yourself up if you miss a target. Remember to treat yourself like your best friend when you face a setback or make a mistake.

To better prepare you for the climb, let's do a recap of the tools and concepts you learned in this book. To do this, here, we will briefly review the main ideas of each chapter.

We started by debunking the notion that procrastination is a modern problem. People have been putting things off since the time of ancient Egyptians! Nevertheless, procrastination has become easier and perhaps more widespread with modern technologies. To get anything done, you should first get started. That is where procrastination becomes an obstacle. Once you start, perhaps you need to deliver a certain output quality. You might be tempted to overdo the task, deliver perfect quality, go beyond expectations, etc. Although striving for excellence is a virtue, but not for every trial task! In real life, you have to be productive, i.e., efficiently finish the tasks that matter the most. The core message of this book is how to get things done by beating procrastination, i.e., getting started and boosting productivity, i.e., finishing tasks off efficiently.

Chapter 1 discussed the psychology of procrastination. The first message was that procrastination is not because of laziness. Similarly, poor time management is not the primary root cause of procrastination. We put things off for various reasons, for example, task aversion, high expectations, distractibility, impulsiveness, and having targets too far in the future. When procrastinating, we prioritize the needs of our present selves over the future ones. We effectively put that task off to be dealt with by our future selves. This is called "Present Bias". Take the snooze button. It has been an exemplar of procrastination. When you hit the snooze button, you tell the day to wait until you are ready for it. You prefer to enjoy sleeping a few minutes more and you being late for a meeting at work is for your future self to handle!

In Chapter 2, we talked about how procrastination manifests itself in daily life. We started with disapproving a few myths about procrastination. For example, any delay is procrastination, or it is in our genes. We procrastinate mainly because the intended task puts us in a lousy mood. By postponing that task, we try to repair our mood and let our future self handle the task. We reviewed some of the common distractors such as our gadgets, noise in the environment, demands from family members, and how to regulate them.

Chapter 3 discussed various procrastination and unproductiveness faces, such as the avoider, the perfectionist, the over-analyzer, and the Busybody. We also reviewed the characteristics of chronic procrastinators and analyzed the role of procrastination in bringing overall productivity down.

Chapter 4 dissected the differences between being busy and being productive. Busy people are often hard-workers, while productive people are more focused on effectiveness, i.e., finding better ways to do things. Productive people are better capable of saying "No", delegate more often, set boundaries for their time and energy, and can deliver the desired results more efficiently. Multitasking is often considered a sign of productivity. However, we saw that only a tiny fraction of multitaskers are genuinely effective in what they do, and we reviewed why that is the case.

Chapter 5 was about perfectionism and how it can become a source of procrastination and prevent us from getting things done because of very high standards, fear of failure, damage to self-worth, and so on. In Chapter 8, the topic of perfectionism was revisited. The focus here was on changing the perfectionist mindset and trying to become more comfortable with embracing imperfection. This change in attitude is crucial to curb perfectionism and disconnect it from our self-worth.

Chapter 6 provided fifteen tools and practices to help you become more productive. If you want to go back and review the productivity tips and tricks, this is your chapter! We discussed a wide range of productivity tools such as the Eisenhower model to determine the importance and urgency, the deep work, delegation, planning and prioritization, journaling, and replenishing your energy.

Chapter 7 discussed the Pareto Principle, also known as the 80/20 principle. This principle's core message is that for most tasks, the link between the inputs (e.g., time and energy) and the outputs is not one to one. For example, fifty percent of your time and effort does not generate fifty percent of the results. In most instances, 20% vital tasks produce roughly 80% of the results. This chapter discussed how to apply the 80/20 principle to boost your productivity by identifying high priority tasks and focusing most of your time and efforts on them while handling the other 80% of the tasks with acceptable quality.

Chapter 9 portrayed a healthy work-life balance as a good measure of having procrastination under control while enjoying high productivity at home and work. The analogy of the acrobat walking on the tightrope juggling balls described what work-life balance could mean in everyday life. This chapter discussed how to combine all the previous chapters' learnings to achieve an outstanding work-life balance and enjoy sustained happiness and productivity.

Chapter 10 focused on internalizing the learnings from previous chapters to sustain and strengthen your new habits when facing setbacks in real life. Using the tools and concepts learned in the earlier chapters combined with the right mindset, realistic view on change, perseverance, and hardiness, you will be on the right path to transforming yourself from a procrastinator into a highly productive person.

Thank you for reading this book! I hope you will enjoy applying your new learnings. You have all the tools to start your exciting journey and soon become a better, more productive version of yourself! If you have enjoyed this book, please take the time to leave a review to help future readers like yourself and help me as an author. Thank you and Good Luck!

RESOURCES

Books

1. "The Science of Overcoming Procrastination: How to Be Disciplined, Break Inertia, Manage Your Time, and Be Productive. Get Off Your Butt and Get Things Done!:, King, P., 2018.

2. "Procrastination: Why You Do It, and What to do About It Now", Burka, J. and Yuen, L., 2008.

3. "Finish: Give Yourself the Gift of Done", Acuff, J., 2018.

4. "Solving the Procrastination Puzzle", Pychyl, T., 2013.

5. "Cure the Procrastination Puzzle with the Power of Habits: Declutter Your Mind with over 7 Highly Effective Atomic Mindset Tricks & Start Mastering Difficult Tasks with Mini Success Lifestyle Changes", Marcus, W.B., Jeffrey A., and Werner B., 2019.

6. The Gifts of Imperfection: Let Go of Who You Think You're Supposed to Be and Embrace Who You Are, Brown, B, 2010.

7. "Perfectionism: A Practical Guide to Managing "Never Good Enough"". Gemert, V.L, 2019.

8. "The Achievement Trap: The Over-Achiever, People-Pleaser, and Perfectionist's Guide to Freedom and True Success. Tebo, B., 2018.

9. "How to Be an Imperfectionist: The New Way to Self-Acceptance, Fearless Living, and Freedom from Perfectionism", Guise, S., 2015.

10. "The Productivity Project: Accomplishing More by Managing Your Time, Attention, and Energy", Bailey.C, 2017

11. "Productivity Is For Robots: How To (re)Connect, Get Creative, And Stay Human In The New World", McComb, C., 2020.

12. "The 7 Habits of Highly Effective People: Powerful Lessons in Personal Change", Covey, S., 2020.

13. "Curating Your Life: Ending the Struggle for Work-Life Balance". Golden, G., 2020

14. "Principles: Life and Work", Dalio, R., 2017.

15. "The 80/20 Principle: The Secret to Success by Achieving More with Less", Koch, R., 2014.

16. Duhigg, C. (2012). *The power of habit: Why we do what we do in life and business.* Random House.

Dissertations, Journal Papers

1. Sirois, F., & Pychyl, T. (2013). Procrastination and the Priority of Short-Term Mood Regulation: Consequences for Future Self. Social and Personality Psychology Compass, 7(2), 115- 127. doi:10.1111/spc3.12011

2. Mischel W. & Shoda Y. Psychological Review 1995, Vol. 102, No. 2, 246-268

3. "Procrastination in Different Life-Domains: Is Procrastination Domain Specific?", Klingsieck, K., 2013, 10.1007/s12144-013-9171-8. Current Psychology

4. "A Relationship of Perfectionism, Rumination and Depression : Adaptive Perfectionism and Maladaptive Perfectionism", Yi, I, 2014, 10.17315/kjhp.2014.19.1.020, Korean Journal of Health Psychology.

5. "Is there an Antidote to Perfectionism", Greenspoon, T., 2014, 10.1002/pits.21797Psychology in the Schools

6. Meng Zhu, Yang Yang, Christopher K Hsee, The Mere Urgency Effect, Journal of Consumer Research, Volume 45, Issue 3, October 2018, Pages 673–690, https://doi.org/10.1093/jcr/ucy008

7. Best, M., & Neuhauser, D. (2006). Joseph Juran: overcoming resistance to organizational change. Quality & safety in health care, 15(5), 380–382.

8. Winter S.G. (2018) Satisficing. In: Augier M., Teece D.J. (eds) The Palgrave Encyclopedia of Strategic Management. Palgrave Macmillan, London. https://doi.org/10.1057/978-1-137-00772-8_594

9. Kross, E., Bruehlman-Senecal, E., Park, J., Burson, A., Dougherty, A., Shablack, H., Bremner, R., Moser, J., & Ayduk, O. (2014). Self-talk as a regulatory mechanism: How you do it matters. *Journal of Personality and Social Psychology.*

10. "Work-life Balance: Is it Now a Problem for Management?", Todd, P. and Binns, J., 2011, 10.1111/j.1468-0432.2011.00564.xGender, Work & Organization

Websites

1. "Procrastination Through the Ages", January 2, 2021, Link: https://www.mentalfloss.com/article/63887/procrastination-through-ages-brief-history-wasting-time

2. "Getting Over Procrastination", January 2, 2021, Link: https://www.newyorker.com/science/maria-konnikova/a-procrastination-gene

3. Psychology of Procrastination: Why People Put Off Important Tasks Until the Last Minute, December 31, 2020, Link:https://www.apa.org/news/press/releases/2010/04/procrastination#:~:text=Dr.,-Ferrari.&text=One%20of%20my%20favorite%20sayings,work%2C%20school%20and%20in%20relationships.

4. "Why Wait? The Science Behind Procrastination", Jaffe, E., March 29, 2013, Psychological Science, Link: https://www.psychologicalscience.org/observer/why-wait-the-science-behind-procrastination.

5. "5 Common Productivity Myths That You Need to Stop Believing, Boogaard, K, January 09, 2018, Link: https://blog.trello.com/5-common-productivity-myths-to-stop-believing

6. "Don't Let Perfectionism be an Enemy of Productivity", Boyes, A., March 03, 2020, Harvard Business Review, Link: https://hbr.org/2020/03/dont-let-perfection-be-the-enemy-of-productivity.

7. "5 Reasons Why Perfectionism Destroys Productivity and What You Can Do About It", Clarke, A., June 6, 2019, Link: https://www.craftyourcontent.com/perfectionism-destroys-productivity/.

8. "The Eisenhower Matrix" December 14, 2020, Link: https://todoist.com/productivity-methods/eisenhower-matrix

9. "Vilfredo Pareto", December 19, 2020, Link: https://www.britannica.com/biography/Vilfredo-Pareto#ref37223

10. "What is Pareto Distribution?", December 19, 2020, Link: https://corporatefinanceinstitute.com/resources/knowledge/economics/pareto-distribution/

11. "Pareto Principle and Parteo Analysis Guide", December 19, 2020, Link : https://www.juran.com/blog/a-guide-to-the-pareto-principle-80-20-rule-pareto-analysis/#:~:text=The%20vital%20few%3A%20A%20small,part%20of%20the%20entire%20problem.

12. "25 Habits of Highly Productive People: Work Smarter, Not Harder".Sisley, C., Workflow, Link: https://www.workflowmax.com/blog/25-habits-of-highly-productive-people-work-smarter-not-harder.

13. "How to Improve Your Work-Life Balance Today", Sanfilippo, M., March 03, 2020, Business News Daily. Link: https://www.businessnewsdaily.com/5244-improve-work-life-balance-today.html

14. "Walking the Work Life Balance Tightrope; A New Way to Setup Your Day", December 26, 2020, Link: https://www.noomii.com/articles/3732-walking-the-work-life-balance-tightrope

15. Brian Dyson's commencement speech in Georgia Tech. in 1991, December 26, 2020, Link: https://www.markturner.net/2015/05/10/text-of-brian-dysons-commencement-speech-at-georgia-tech-sept-1991/

16. "5 Reasons Why Maintaining a Worl-Life Balance is So Important", Trivett, C., Coburg Banks. Link: https://www.coburgbanks.co.uk/blog/candidate-tips/importance-of-maintaining-work-life-balance/

17. "Work-Life Balance Defined", December 27, 2020, Link: https://worklifebalance.com/work-life-balance-defined/

18. "Mental health in the workplace", December 27, 2020, Link https://www.euro.who.int/en/health-topics/noncommunicable-diseases/mental-health/areas-of-work/mental-health-in-the-workplace

19. "Warren Buffett Says You'll Be a Wreck if You Don't Take Care of Your Mind and Body", December 27, 2020, Link: https://www.inc.com/marcel-schwantes/warren-buffett-says-when-it-comes-to-your-future-success-dont-neglect-these-2-things-or-youll-be-a-wreck.html

20. "The 80/20 Rule Explained", Brian Tracy International. Link: https://www.briantracy.com/blog/personal-success/how-to-use-the-80-20-rule-pareto-principle/

21. "The Tricks that Can Turn You Into a Speed Reader", Hammond, C., December 2, 2019, BBC.com. Link: https://www.bbc.com/future/article/20191129-how-to-learn-to-speed-read

22. "How to use the 80/20 Rule to Change Your Life", Erin Gobler. Link: https://eringobler.com/80-20-rule/

23. "6 Surefire Ways to Survive Crunch Time", Gillell-Stuy, S.. Link: https://susangilellstuy.com/2018/01/6-surefire-ways-to-survive-crunch-time/

24. "The man who kicked our butts", December 30, 2020, Link: https://www.ft.com/content/1c09c0a8-1d6b-11e2-869b-00144feabdc0

25. "Apollo Fight Journal: Day 6, part 4: The Last Course Correction", December 30, 2020 Link: https://history.nasa.gov/afj/ap13fj/25day6-thelastcoursecorrection.html

26. "Rock Climbing: A Metaphor For Achieving Your Goal", January 2, 2021, Link: https://medium.com/@ericmartel/rock-climbing-a-metaphor-for-achieving-your-goal-b786b424f6fa

www.ingramcontent.com/pod-product-compliance
Lightning Source LLC
Chambersburg PA
CBHW021424070526
44577CB00001B/46